Malakhovs Dornröschen

Malakhovs Dornröschen

Seitensprünge
mit dem Staatsballett Berlin

Frank Sistenich und
Christiane Theobald (Hrsg.)

Fotografien
von Monika Rittershaus

SCHOTT

Bibliografische Information der Deutschen Bibliothek
Die Deutsche Bibliothek verzeichnet diese Publikation in der
Deutschen Nationalbibliografie; detaillierte bibliografische
Daten sind im Internet über http://dnb.ddb.de abrufbar.

Ausgabe mit deutschem Umschlag
Bestellnummer ED 9965
ISBN 3-7957-0544-4

English jacket Edition
Product number 9965-01
ISBN 3-7957-0557-6

Englische Textfassung: Esther Dubielzig

© 2006 Schott Musik International GmbH & Co. KG, Mainz

www.schott-music.com
www.staatsballett-berlin.de

Alle Rechte vorbehalten
Nachdruck in jeder Form sowie die Wiedergabe durch Fernsehen,
Rundfunk, Film, Bild- und Tonträger oder Benutzung für Vorträge,
auch auszugsweise, nur mit Genehmigung des Verlags

Umschlaggestaltung: Hans Spörri unter Verwendung
eines Fotos von Monika Rittershaus
Grafik-Design: Hans Spörri
Druckformenherstellung: typossatz GmbH Berlin
Druck und buchbinderische Verarbeitung:
freiburger graphische betriebe GmbH & Co. KG

Printed in Germany · BSS 52043

Inhalt

7   Grußwort von Vladimir Malakhov

8   Prolog

10   Essay

22   Die Besetzung

23   Die Handlung

25   Akt 1

79   Akt 2

113   Akt 3

Content

7   Greeting by Vladimir Malakhcv

9   Prologue

16   Essay

22   The cast

23   The plot

25   Act 1

79   Act 2

113   Act 3

Träume und Visionen

Träume und Visionen bestimmen unser Leben. Sie machen uns alle innerlich reich, stimmen optimistisch und lassen uns hoffen. Träumen wir nicht alle manchmal davon, dass etwas geschieht, das unser Leben auf wundersame Weise verändert?

Dornröschen, die Sleeping Beauty, ist die Märchen gewordene Form solcher Träume. Ich hatte immer eine genaue Vorstellung von meinem *Dornröschen*-Traum und ich bin sehr froh, dass ich ihn mit dem Staatsballett Berlin für Sie wahr machen durfte. In Berlin habe ich mit meiner Compagnie die Bedingungen und das Glück gefunden, mich meinem Traum zu widmen. Wie dies geschah und wie wir alle gemeinsam daran gearbeitet haben, davon erzählt Ihnen das vorliegende Buch.

Ihr Vladimir Malakhov

Dreams and visions

Dreams and visions define our lives. They all fill us with inner wealth, make us feel optimistic and give us hope. Don't we all dream sometimes that something may happen that will change our lives in a wondrous way?

The Sleeping Beauty is such a dream which has turned into a fairy-tale. I always had a clear picture of my *Sleeping Beauty* dream in my mind, and I am very glad that I was able to make it come true for you with the Berlin State Ballet. In Berlin, with my company, I found the conditions and the luck to realize my dream. How this happened and how we all worked on it together is told in this book.

Yours Vladimir Malakhov

Prolog

Wer sehnt sich nicht danach, wach geküsst zu werden? Die zentrale Erlösungsmetapher so vieler Märchen ist in Berlin Wirklichkeit geworden. Mit der Gründung des Staatsballetts Berlin unter der Intendanz von Vladimir Malakhov haben sich Partner gefunden, die wie füreinander geschaffen sind. Wahlverwandtschaften scheinen es gewesen zu sein, die die Fusion der ehemaligen Ballette der drei Berliner Opernhäuser der Staatsoper Unter den Linden, der Deutschen Oper und der Komischen Oper zur größten Ballettcompagnie der Bundesrepublik fügten. Keine Dornenhecke schien zu dicht, als dass sie nicht überwunden zu werden lohnte. In der Erwartung des Prinzen schlief es sich einstmals gut und nur der Richtige durfte es sein, der die Ruhe zu stören und die Vision zu leben wagt. Mit Malakhov ist das Staatsballett Berlin zu neuem Leben erwacht, ein Erweckungskuss mit Folgen sozusagen. Wer den Preis der Schönsten aller Schlafenden begehrt, darf das Risiko nicht scheuen. Was liegt da näher auf der Hand als die Wahl von Tschaikovskys *Dornröschen* als große Choreographiearbeit von Vladimir Malakhov für seine Berliner Compagnie? Dieser Meilenstein der Ballettliteratur ist Anlass für den vorliegenden Bildband, die spürbare Leidenschaft der Solisten des Staatsballetts Berlin und seines Intendanten zu dokumentieren.

Was wir ohne Leidenschaft tun, gerät auch danach. Nur Leidenschaft wirkt authentisch und bildet die Voraussetzung für das Publikum, sich mit der Compagnie und ihren Idolen zu identifizieren. Leidenschaft zieht uns an, sie bindet und verbindet. Sie berührt unsere Seele und trifft ins Herz. Und ach, gelegentlich entblößt sie uns. Wer erinnert sich nicht an die vielen Abende leidenschaftlicher Eindrücke, die Tanz und Tänzer in uns hinterlassen haben? Unsere Waffen wurden gestreckt, gleich an der Garderobe. Wir sind gekommen, uns zu ergeben. Freiwillig und mit höchster Lust. Doch auch hier gilt: kein Eindruck ohne Ausdruck. Der leidenschaftliche Ausdruck bedingt ein Tänzerleben, das sich auch jenseits der für uns alle sichtbaren Bühnenpräsenz behaupten muss. Das Erhabene und das Profane, beides gehört auch zum Alltag des Tänzers und beides liegt, wie so oft und so vieles in unserem Leben, eng beieinander. Es sind die Seitensprünge jenseits der Bühne und des Blickes, den wir von ihr haben, die den Höhepunkt der Aufführung vorbereiten und möglich machen. Ob professioneller Trainingsalltag oder die privaten Momente der Ein- und Zweisamkeit. Beide bilden den Rahmen, aus dem der Tänzer hinaus auf die Bühne zu springen hat, um sich unserer Aufmerksamkeit zu versichern. In diesem wahrsten Sinne des Wortes ist die allabendliche *Dornröschen*-Vorstellung für den Gast eine geschlossene Veranstaltung. Die Perspektive des Bildbandes ist eine Einladung, gemeinsam mit den Solisten des Staatsballetts Berlin und Vladimir Malakhov aus diesem Rahmen herauszutreten und sie bei ihren alltäglichen Seitensprüngen während der *Dornröschen*-Produktion zu begleiten. Werfen wir also einen Blick auf die sonst verborgenen und privaten Augenblicke, ohne die es die einzigartigen Bühnenmomente für uns alle nicht gäbe.

Wer den Seitensprung wagt, muss sich seines Weges sicher sein. Wer vom Pfad abkommt, verirrt sich in den Dornen und lebt gefährlich. Seitensprünge sind konstitutiv, um den eigenen Weg fortsetzen zu können. Sie fordern heraus, sind als neue Erfahrung das Salz in der Suppe des Alltags und leisten oft erst die notwendige Orientierung, den eigenen Standpunkt zu bestimmen. Und es soll sogar vorkommen, dass der Seitensprung als schönste Nebensache sich rasch zur Hauptaufgabe entwickelt. *Vie experimentale* heißt die Devise. Läge Dornröschen nicht heute noch hinter der großen Hecke verborgen, wenn sich die Prinzen ihrer Zeit den verschlungenen Wegen verweigert hätten? ›Wer nicht wagt, der nicht gewinnt‹, lernen wir sprichwörtlich für die Eroberungen unseres Lebens. In jedem Fall gilt: Nur wer praktisch aus dem Rahmen zu springen versteht, wird diesen auch zu schätzen wissen. Die Berliner *Dornröschen*-Produktion zeigt Vladimir Malakhov als Prinzen Désiré inmitten seines eigenen Ensembles. Der Jahrhunderttänzer feiert Premiere und widmet sich als Choreograph damit erstmals der Doppelrolle des ersten Solisten wie auch des leitenden Intendanten des Staatsballetts Berlin. Die schlafende Schöne schläft nicht mehr, Braut und Bräutigam sind vereint und feiern Triumphe. Das Warten hat sich gelohnt, und die Welt schaut mit gespannter Erwartung nach Berlin. Dornröschen nimmt schließlich nicht jeden. Warum sollte sie auch? Sie schlief ja gut, träumte tief und fest vor sich hin. So, wie auch nicht jeder Prinz bereit war, sich um ihrer Willen durch die Dornenhecke zu schlagen. Der Richtige muss es also jeweils sein, für beide Partner, und er ist es geworden. Alle, die mit von der Partie sind, laden Sie nun ein, einen Blick in den Mikrokosmos des Staatsballetts Berlin zu werfen. Einen *pas d'action* mit Leserbeteiligung wollen wir wagen. Gemeinsam mit der Berliner Fotografin Monika Rittershaus erzählen uns Prinz Désiré und Dornröschen von ihrem Glück. Ihr und der gesamten Compagnie gilt dafür unser herzlicher Dank. Wie gerne erwarten wir als Prinz oder Prinzessin den Erlösungskuss des richtigen Partners im Leben, und in dieser Hoffnung scheinen selbst 100 Jahre Einsamkeit fast ohne Belang. In Berlin wird viel geküsst in diesen Tagen …

Frank Sistenich und Christiane Theobald

Prologue

Who does not long to be woken with a kiss? The central salvation metaphor of so many fairy-tales has come true in Berlin. The foundation of the Berlin State Ballet under the direction of Vladimir Malakhov has brought together partners who are perfect for each other. It seems to have been elective affinities that had the former ballets of the three Berlin opera houses (the State Opera Unter den Linden, the Deutsche Oper and the Komische Oper) join together to form the largest ballet company of Germany. No thorn hedge seemed to be so dense as to not be worth being overcome. In expectation of the prince, sleep once was peaceful, and only Mr Right was supposed to disturb this peace and live the vision. Malakhov has revived the Berlin State Ballet, it was a kiss of awakening fraught with consequences, so to speak. Who desires the most beautiful of all sleeping beauties as a price, must not be afraid of danger and risk. What could be more natural for Vladimir Malakhov than choosing Tchaikovsky's *Sleeping Beauty* as great choreography project for his Berlin company? This milestone in ballet literature is featured in this illustrated book documenting the noticeable passion of the soloists of the Berlin State Ballet and its director.

What is done dispassionately, turns out to be without passion. But only passion appears authentic, providing the foundation for the audience's identification with the company and their idols. It is passion that attracts, binds and links us. It touches our soul and affects us deeply. And, alas, sometimes it even reveals our selves. Who does not remember the numerous evenings of passionate impressions left by dancers and dances? We admit defeat – right at the cloakroom. We have come to surrender. Of our own free will and with the greatest pleasure. But even here it holds true that there is no impression without expression. Passionate expression is associated with a dancer's life which has to survive even beyond its presence on the stage where it is visible to all of us. The sublime and the mundane – both are part of a dancer's daily life and both are never far apart, as is so often the case in our lives. It is the escapades outside the stage and our view of the stage that prepare the climax of the performance and make it possible. No matter whether professional training routine or private moments of solitude and togetherness. Both form the framework out of which the dancer has to jump on the stage to secure our attention. For the guests,the regular evening performance of *The Sleeping Beauty* is a closed event in the truest sense of the word. The perspective of this illustrated book is an invitation to step out of this framework with the soloists of the Berlin State Ballet and Vladimir Malakhov and accompany them throughout their daily escapades during the production of *The Sleeping Beauty*. Let us have a look at the normally hidden and private moments without which there would not be any of those great unforgettable moments for us on the stage.

Who dares to have any escapades, has to be sure of his path. Who loses his way, gets lost in the thorns and lives a dangerous life. Escapades are constitutive, in the sense that they help to continue one's own path. They are challenges and, as a new experience, the icing on the cake of everyday life, often providing the necessary orientation to define one's own standpoint. It may even happen that the escapade as the most delightful trivial pursuit in the world quickly develops into the most important thing. Our motto is *vie experimentale*. Wouldn't the Sleeping Beauty still be hidden behind the large hedge if the princes of her time had refused to follow the intricate paths? Nothing ventured, nothing gained – this is what we literally learn for the conquests of our lives. In any case, it holds true that only he who knows how to jump out of the framework will appreciate it. The Berlin production of *The Sleeping Beauty* shows Vladimir Malakhov as Prince Désiré in the midst of his own ensemble. The exceptional dancer makes his debut as a choreographer, thus acting for the first time in the dual capacity of principal soloist and artistic director of the Berlin State Ballet. The Sleeping Beauty is no longer sleeping, bride and groom are united and achieve great triumphs. The wait has been worth its while, and the world is looking at Berlin with great expectations. After all, the Sleeping Beauty does not take just anybody. Why should she? She slept well, dreaming soundly and safely. Just as not each prince was willing to cut his way through the thorn hedge for her sake. It has to be the right person, for both partners, and he has been found. All those who have had a part in this production invite you to have a look at the microcosmos of the Berlin State Ballet. Together with the readers, we want to try a *pas d'action*. Supported by the Berlin photographer Monika Rittershaus, Prince Désiré and the Sleeping Beauty tell us the story of their love. We would like to give our special thanks to her and the entire company. We, too, as prince or princess, hope for the kiss of salvation from the right partner in life, and it is this hope that makes even 100 years of solitude appear to be of almost no importance. There is a lot of kissing in Berlin these days …

Frank Sistenich and Christiane Theobald

Malakhovs *Dornröschen* für das Staatsballett Berlin

Dornröschen, eine Erfolgsgeschichte

Der Wunsch, in Superlativen zu denken, scheint nicht nur ein Kind unserer Zeit zu sein. Bereits Tschaikowsky stellte zu *Dornröschen* fest, es sei sein bestes und geglücktestes Ballett. Ihm gehöre die Krone seines Schaffens, ein Funkeln von kunstvoll geschliffenen Edelsteinen. So gilt es für Choreographen und Tänzer jeder Zeit, sich diesem Schatz zu widmen, ihn zu polieren und damit immer wieder dem Publikum in seiner schönsten Form vorzustellen. Komponisten, Generationen von Tänzern und auch das Publikum stimmen unisono überein und schätzen Tschaikowskys *Dornröschen* als eines der schönsten und prächtigsten Ballette der Tanzliteratur überhaupt. Wo finden wir ein solches einstimmiges Urteil sonst in der Welt der großen Kunst? Igor Strawinsky schrieb: ›Ich habe wieder einmal die Partitur dieses Ballettes gelesen! (…) und habe einige Tage lang das Vergnügen genossen, darin immer wieder dasselbe Gefühl der Frische, des Erfindungsgeistes, der Genialität und der Lebendigkeit zu finden.‹ Und er wünschte sich ›von Herzen‹, dass das Publikum ›aus allen Ländern dieses Werk ebenso empfindet, wie es von mir, einem russischen Musiker, empfunden wird.‹ Und Rudolf Nurejew stellte gar fest: ›*Dornröschen* ist das Ballett der Ballette. Schon meine erste Lehrerin nannte es immer die Königin der Ballette.‹ Bis in unsere Tage hinein weiß das Publikum um die elementare Wirkung dieses Klassikers.

So umfassend heute die Erfolgsgeschichte *Dornröschen* auch anmuten mag, zu Anfang hat es nicht danach ausgesehen, dass Tschaikowsky mit diesem Ballett das Schlüsselwerk und die Quintessenz seines Schaffens vorlegen würde. Seine erste große Ballettmusik, *Schwanensee*, war bereits 1875/76 geschrieben, aber dem Ballett war leider nach den ersten Moskauer Aufführungen kein unmittelbar durchschlagender Erfolg beschieden. *Schwanensee* galt als unprätentiöses Werk mit alten Bühnenbildern und Kostümen, die ad hoc zusammengestellt wurden. Obwohl die Musik bereits einen für das Genre des klassischen Balletts ungewöhnlich begabten Sinfoniker erkennen ließ, hatte Tschaikowsky das Thema Ballettmusik ad acta gelegt, er zog sich zurück und widmete sich anderen Musikgattungen. Im Mai 1888 hatte allerdings der herausragende Theaterdirektor der Kaiserlichen Theater St. Petersburg, Iwan A. Wsewoloschski, der das Talent Tschaikowskys schon früh erkannt hatte, ›den Wunsch, ein Libretto nach der Erzählung von Perrault *Die Schöne, die im Walde schlief*, zu schreiben. Die Idee möchte ich im Stile Ludwig des XIV. gestalten.… Im letzten Akt ist eine Quadrille über alle Perrault'schen Erzählungen unbedingt nötig.‹ (aus einem Brief Wsewoloschskis an Tschaikowsky vom 13. Mai 1888). Die Idee zum Ballett *Dornröschen* war geboren. Dass dieses ein solcher Erfolg wurde, ist zu einem großen Teil Wsewoloschski und seinem großen Interesse für Ballett zuzuschreiben. Als Theaterdirektor kannte er die Bedürfnisse der Kunstform nur zu gut. Sein Engagement für Tschaikowskys Bühnenwerke war grenzenlos, und er muss zudem ein interessanter Mann gewesen sein, mit einem scharfen Geist, mit Stil und Raffinement. All dies hat Tschaikowsky gefallen, und es war die Voraussetzung für die wunderbare Zusammenarbeit zwischen Wsewoloschski, Tschaikowsky und Petipa, aus der die erste großartige *Dornröschen*-Produktion entstanden ist. Wsewoloschski war derart engagiert, dass er allein 221 Kostümfigurinen für das Ballett geliefert hat. Die stilistischen Möglichkeiten des Projektes in der Kombination dieser drei Protagonisten waren es, die den Komponisten schnell überzeugten. Im August desselben Jahres erhielt Tschaikowsky bereits das Libretto seines Theaterdirektors und war ›unbeschreiblich bezaubert und entzückt‹. In vollkommener Weise fügte es sich in die Tradition der Ballett-Feerien ein, die zu dieser Zeit in Russland so beliebt waren. Wsewoloschski hat die Perrault'sche Erzählung einer Bearbeitung unterzogen, den Anforderungen des Zarenhofes nach prunkvoller Unterhaltung entsprochen und dabei nicht vergessen, dem Zaren die unterschwellig erwarteten Schmeicheleien zu bieten. Die Handlung bildete nun eine gekürzte und redigierte Version des Volksmärchens, eine Handlung, in deren Rahmen sich die Kunst des klassischen Balletts – dargestellt in verschiedenen großen Divertissements – mit all ihren Möglichkeiten entfalten konnte. Am 25. Juli 1889, während der Arbeit an der Instrumentierung der Partitur, schrieb Tschaikowsky an Frau von Meck: ›Der Stoff ist so poetisch, so lohnend für die Musik, dass ich von dem Ballett ganz gefesselt war und mit einem Eifer und einer Hingabe schrieb, wie sie die beste Voraussetzung für das Gelingen einer Komposition sind.‹

Das Libretto ist so angelegt, dass der Zuschauer bereits am Ende des Prologs weiß, wie sich die Geschichte weiterentwickelt. Spektakuläre Tanzszenen als Kompensation für eine weniger wichtige Handlung ist das Charakteristikum der Ballett-Feerien, und so denkt jeder heutzutage bei *Dornröschen* an herrliche Musik und prachtvolle Choreografie. ›Wenn man die dramatische Struktur von *Dornröschen* an den Erfordernissen des Sprechtheaters misst, dann erscheint diese dürftig und außerordentlich langatmig. Auch für eine Oper wäre sie eintönig und langweilig. Aber weil die Prinzipien der sinfonischen Handlungsentwicklung beachtet werden, ist sie als Basis für ein Ballett geradezu ideal‹ (Vera Krasowskaja, Dornröschen – ein Schlüsselwerk der Ballettgeschichte). Tschaikowsky selbst bemerkte einmal, ins Ballett primär der Handlung wegen zu gehen, sei vergleichbar mit dem Wunsch, die Oper der Rezitative wegen aufzusuchen. Für den Komponisten Tschaikowsky steht die Form von *Dornröschen* als seinem besten Ballett der Sinfonie näher als der des Dramas und auch Marius Petipa, der Choreograph, legte mit *Dornröschen* sein opus magnum vor. ›Dornröschen‹ ist das stärkste und am höchsten vervollkommnete Werk Petipas; es fasst die lange, schwierige und hartnäckige Suche des Choreographen nach der Synthese von Sinfonie und Ballett gewissermaßen zusammen‹ (Vera Krasowskaja). Petipa orientierte sich an den herrschenden Konstruktionsprinzipien, indem er das Ballett in eine konventionelle Pantomime zur Verdeutlichung der Handlung einerseits und in den klassischen Tanz zum Ausdruck der Affekte andererseits unterteilte. Bereits über siebzig Jahre alt, liefert auch der Choreograph sein Meisterstück ab und krönt nicht nur sein eigenes künstlerisches Schaffen. Petipas *Dornröschen* wird zum Inbegriff des Stils einer ganzen Epoche, der Aufführungen ›à grand ballet‹. Bis zu diesem Zeitpunkt am 3. Januar 1890 hatte die Welt noch kein vollkommeneres Ballett gesehen. ›Mir scheint, dass es eine Harmonie geschaffen hat, eine in ihrer Art einmalige Harmonie zwischen dem Choreographen, dem Komponisten dem Bühnenausstatter und den Darstellern (…). Dies ist auch Tschaikowskys vollkommenstes, choreografiegerechtestes Ballett. Eine unerklärbare Wärme und Heiterkeit sind der Musik eigen, eine ganz besondere, sich nirgends wiederholende Klangharmonie, die uns in eine erstaunliche, märchenhafte Welt führt‹ (Leonid. W. Jakobson, Petipas Geheimnis).

Die Musik von Peter I. Tschaikowsky

Als Peter I. Tschaikowsky später einmal die eigentliche Kompositionsdauer, von der Orchestrierung einmal abgesehen, zusammenrechnete, fand er heraus, dass er diese wunderbaren, knapp drei Stunden Musik in nur vierzig Tagen geschrieben hatte. Auf der letzten Seite des Particells hat Tschaikowsky vermerkt: ›Ich habe den Entwurf am 26. Mai 1889 um 8 Uhr vollendet. Gelobt sei Gott! Insgesamt habe ich zehn Tage im Oktober, drei Wochen im Januar und jetzt eine Woche daran gearbeitet.‹ Tschaikowsky muss außerordentlich motiviert gewesen sein, sicher auch durch die glückliche Fügung des Dreigestirns der Protagonisten, die hauptsächlich für dieses Projekt verantwortlich zeichneten. Am 13. August schrieb er erneut an seine Mäzenin und Vertraute Frau von Meck: ›Ich habe mit besonderer Sorgfalt und Liebe an der Instrumentierung gearbeitet und einige ganz neue Kombinationen für das Orchester gewählt, die, wie ich hoffe, sehr schön und interessant sein werden.‹ Ein wahres Feuerwerk leichter, glitzernder Farben entzündet Tschaikowsky im Rahmen eines minutiös vertonten Tanzprogramms. Der Komponist hat Petipas Angaben in Musik übertragen, er hat die dramatische Entwicklung der

Handlung in musikalische Bewegung übersetzt und eine exzellente Balance in engster Absprache mit dem Choreographen Petipa zwischen Pantomime und klassischem Tanz geschaffen. ›Bevor er an die Arbeit ging, bat er den Ballettmeister Marius Petipa, die Tänze, die Zahl der Takte, den Charakter der Musik, die Dauer jeder Nummer aufs genaueste zu bezeichnen.‹ (Modest Tschaikowsky, Das Leben Peter I. Tschaikowskys).

Bereits in seinem Ballett *Schwanensee* hat Tschaikowsky Leitthemen verwendet und den zentralen Rollen im Werk zugeordnet. Im Fall von *Dornröschen* nimmt der Komponist den Faden der leitmotivischen Arbeit wieder auf und konzipiert auf diese Weise die musikalischen wie auch dramatischen Hauptfiguren des Balletts: Nicht Aurora oder Prinz Désiré stehen hier im Mittelpunkt der akustischen Aufmerksamkeit, sondern die gute Fliederfee und die böse Fee Carabosse. Beide Feen haben ihre Leitmotive zur Begleitung ihres Erscheinens auf der Bühne, um im musikalischen Geschehen von ihren Absichten zu künden. Über Petipas Choreografie heißt es entsprechend: ›Obwohl Prinzessin Aurora und Prinz Désiré als Haupthelden in *Dornröschen* gelten und gerade sie mit einer Fülle klassischen Tanzes ausgestattet sind, bleiben dennoch die Fee Carabosse und die Fliederfee die zentralen, die Handlung bewegenden Figuren. Und wenn die Fliederfee sehr einfach angelegt war (…), so ist die Fee Carabosse – eine tänzerisch-pantomimische Figur – vollkommen‹ (Leonid W. Jakobson, Petipas Geheimnis). Diese Struktur hat auch Vladimir Malakhov übernommen, in dem er in seiner Choreografie diese beide Feen in das Zentrum der Aktion rückte.

Zu den glühendsten Verehrern der Werke Petipas gehörte Michail Fokin, der für Diaghilews Ballets Russes choreografierte. Russische Tänzer haben immer wieder Ausschnitte aus *Dornröschen* in den beiden ersten Jahrzehnten des 20. Jahrhunderts auch außerhalb von Russland gezeigt, doch die erste denkwürdige Inszenierung jenseits der Grenzen Russlands ging 1921 als *Sleeping Princess* in London mit Diaghilews Ballets Russes über die Bühne. Léon Bakst schuf seinerzeit die märchenhafte Ausstattung. Igor Strawinsky, der an der musikalischen Vorbereitung beteiligt war, schrieb am 18. Oktober einen berühmt gewordenen offenen Brief an Serge Diaghilew in *The Times* und schloss mit den Worten: ›Es freut mich sehr, dass ich an dieser Aufführung mitarbeiten konnte, denn ich liebe Tschaikowsky; aber ich bewundere auch das klassische Ballett, die Schönheit seiner Ordnung und die aristokratische Strenge seiner Form. Seine Haltung entspricht vollkommen der Auffassung, die ich von der Kunst habe. Im klassischen Tanz sehe ich den Triumph maßvoller Planung über das schweifende Gefühl, der Regel über die Willkür, der Ordnung über den »Zufall«.‹

Tschaikowsky war ein Neuerer der Ballettmusik, er befreite das Ballett aus den Händen eines Ludwig Minkus und übertrug seine sinfonischen Ansprüche auch auf die Komposition für das Ballett, ein Impuls, der später von Igor Strawinsky weiterentwickelt wurde. Rhythmus, Orchestrierung und tonale Struktur wurden von Tschaikowsky auf einem neuen Niveau behandelt. In seiner Ballettmusik wird deutlich, wie er es verstand, die Bedürfnisse des Choreographen mit seinen eigenen als Komponist in Einklang zu bringen. Ballettmusik war mit einem Mal grundlegend sinfonischer gestaltet. Am 28. Februar 1889 schrieb Tschaikowsky an seinen Verleger P. I. Jurgenson: ›Sicherlich sind sich Ballett und Symphonie ähnlich.‹ Tschaikowsky leistete die bis zu diesen Zeitpunkt fortschrittlichste Synthese zwischen Sinfonie und Ballettmusik. Der nicht selten zitierte Vorwurf, Tschaikowskys Musik sei süßlich, greift dagegen ins Leere und wirft eher ein Licht auf die subjektive Rezipientendisposition als auf die objektive Güte der Komposition selbst. Man kann in diesem Zusammenhang ein Bonmot von Sergiu Celibidache über Rimski-Korsakow zitieren, der einmal feststellte, dass derjenige, der diese Musik als zu süßlich empfinde, seinen Diabetes immer schon in die Aufführung mitbringe. ›Tschaikowskys Musik ist wunderbar und das ganze Märchen ist bereits darin enthalten. Tänzer lieben Tschaikowsky dafür, man braucht nur noch zu tanzen‹ (Vladimir Malakhov).

Die Autorität Tschaikowskys vermochte auch den Choreographen Marius Petipa zu einer wirklichen Zusammenarbeit zu bewegen. ›Petipa achtete Tschaikowsky aufs Höchste und wenn er ihn nicht fürchtete, so schätze er doch die Zusammenarbeit mit ihm. Angesichts des hochgesteckten Ziels war jedes Detail bedeutend. Natürlich verlangte Petipa von Tschaikowsky nicht, was er von weniger bedeutenden Komponisten verlangt hätte, aber was Tschaikowsky ihm geben konnte, ergriff der Ballettmeister mit der ihm eigenen Energie‹ (Vera Krasowskaja, Dornröschen – ein Schlüsselwerk der Ballettgeschichte). Die Zusammenarbeit zwischen beiden Künstlern in der Hochzeit der Entstehung des Balletts war vorbildhaft und rundum synergetisch. Auch wenn die historischen Quellen der Zeitzeugen über die Reibungslosigkeit der Zusammenarbeit zwischen den beiden Künstlern nicht immer einig sind, ist durch sie ein Glücksfall für das Ballettrepertoire dokumentiert, wie es später nur noch einmal zwischen Strawinsky und verschiedenen Choreographen gelungen ist. Die außerordentlich reiche Instrumentationspalette, der ausgewogene Bau aus Szenen, Tänzen und Divertissements, die Formenvielfalt und der musikalische Gedankenreichtum sind im Verhältnis von Quantität und Qualität bis heute nicht wieder erreicht worden. ›Der russische Stil der Musik, wie Tschaikowsky ihn so kraftvoll in den letzten Jahren vertrat, wird immer wieder spürbar. Die Musik passt völlig zu den Kostümen und dem Charakter des Stücks; sie besitzt eine französische Nuance, schmeckt aber gleichzeitig russisch. Was immer auch andere empfinden mögen, ich bin in diese französische Geschichte, die von russischer Musik begleitet wird, leidenschaftlich verliebt‹ (Herrman A. Laroche, Peter I. Tschaikowsky)

Malakhovs Version für Berlin und die zentrale Rolle der Feen

Vladimir Malakhov steht in direkter Tradition zu den Urhebern der Ballett-Feerie *Dornröschen*: Petipa und Tschaikowsky. Er ist seit seiner Ausbildung in Moskau mit Tschaikowsky und *Dornröschen* aufgewachsen und hat bis heute weit über 100 Mal die Rolle des Prinzen Désiré in diversen Produktionen über den Globus verteilt getanzt. Und zudem stand auch seine Berliner Tanzpremiere unter dem Stern dieses Prachtballetts. Im Jahr 1995 verkörperte er Prinz Désiré in der legendären Fassung von Rudolf Nurejew auf der Bühne der Staatsoper Unter den Linden. Von diesem Zeitpunkt an kam er regelmäßig als Gast nach Berlin, bis er sich 2002 überzeugen ließ, die künstlerische Leitung des Balletts der Staatsoper zu übernehmen und schließlich seit 2004 als Intendant des Staatsballetts Berlin die Geschicke des mit 88 Tänzerinnen und Tänzern größten Ballettensembles Deutschlands zu leiten.

Die Bilder- und Märchenwelt der französisch anmutenden Ballett-Feerie hat Malakhov immer schon fasziniert und so war es nicht verwunderlich, dass er eine eigene Version des ›Balletts aller Ballette‹ anstrebte. Malakhov hat das extrem lange Werk auf gute zwei Stunden gekürzt. Dabei ging ihm Alexander Sotnikov hilfreich zur Hand, der auch die musikalische Leitung der Produktion innehatte. Sotnikov ist ein genauer Kenner der Ballettpartituren Tschaikowskys, der die vielen verschiedenen Fassungen des *Dornröschens* aufgeführt hat und ein versierter Berater für jede Kürzung und Umstellung der Partitur. Im Unterschied zur klassischen Vorlage ändert Malakhov das *Setting*, in dem er es deutlich mehr der kongenialen Musik Tschaikowskys anpasst. Der sehr farbenreichen Instrumentierung der Partitur wird durch eine Transformation der Handlung in einen blühenden Rosengarten entsprochen. Das Märchen spielt also nicht mehr in einem alten Schloss, sondern quasi unter freiem Himmel inmitten von Mutter Natur. Es ist ein magischer Garten, ein *Hortus conclusus*, nur von Rosenbüschen und Rosenhecken umgeben. Malakhov ist ein leidenschaftlicher Blumenliebhaber. ›Rosen geben meinem *Dornröschen* die Atmosphäre. Sie sind wirklich überall. Und es werden im Verlauf des Abends immer mehr, denn die Rosenhecke wächst von Akt zu Akt. Man muss sehen können, wie sie duften.‹ Die Blumen haben Blüten und Dornen. Auch hier treffen unmittelbar über die Bühnenraumgestaltung die gute und die böse Welt zusammen. Die Dornen der Rose sind ein Symbol für den Schmerz, aber auch für die Angst. Die Dornenhecke, hinter der Dornröschen seinen hundertjährigen Schlaf verbringt, steht für Schutz einerseits, aber auch für Trennung und die Hoffnung auf Erlösung.

Der zentrale Akzent des Ballettes in der Fassung von Malakhov betrifft die Rolle der Fliederfee. In Nurejews Version von *Dornröschen* ist diese Partie eine Schreitrolle. In der Berliner Malakhov-Produktion ist die Fliederfee fast immer auf der Bühne präsent, sie tanzt auf Spitze und hat großartige Variationen zu der Musik, die in der Urfassung dem Solo des Prinzen vorbehalten war. Eine große Freude für jede Tänzerin dieser Rolle, die immer davon geträumt hat, einmal zu dieser Musik tanzen zu können. Die gute Fliederfee hat die Eigenschaften der Demut und Nächstenliebe verinnerlicht, ohne sie ist kein Happy End denkbar, ohne sie gäbe es keine Erlösung. Es wird an ihr sein, den unerschrockenen Prinzen zu dem schlafenden Dornröschen zu geleiten.

Die Gegenspielerin der guten Fliederfee, die böse Fee Carabosse (sie wurde bereits in der Uraufführung von einem Mann getanzt), personifiziert die dunklen Seiten des Lebens. Da man vergessen hatte, die Fee Carabosse als eine von zahlreichen Feen, die ihre guten Wünsche aussprechen, zur Taufe von Prinzessin Aurora einzuladen, verhängt diese einen bösen Fluch über das Neugeborene: Aurora wird sich stechen und daran sterben. Doch die gute Fliederfee verhindert das Schlimmste, indem sie den Fluch abmildert. Dem Stich – auf der Berliner Bühne durch eine vergiftete Rose, nicht die ursprüngliche Spindel – wird ein hundertjähriger Schlaf hinter einer Dornenhecke folgen und nur durch den Kuss eines Prinzen, der die Dornenhecke durchdringt, kann die schlafende Aurora wieder zu Leben erweckt werden. Das Besondere der Berliner *Dornröschen*-Produktion liegt darin, dass Malakhov auch dieser Rolle im Vergleich zur Urfassung einen höheren Stellenwert einräumt, indem Carabosse das Schlusstableau mitbestimmt, im Hochzeitsbild daher noch einmal ihren Auftritt hat und den Fluss der glücklich endenden Handlung zum Stocken bringt. Ihr gehört im letzten Bild eine Generalpause und alle Aufmerksamkeit von Publikum und Akteuren. An dieser Stelle sinnt sie auf die Revanche, das Gute und das Böse treffen mit der Fee Carabosse und der Fliederfee noch einmal aufeinander und bis zur Coda konkurrieren sie nicht nur leitmotivisch im Orchestergraben, sondern ebenso über ihren Tanz auf der Bühne, sie lenken und leiten die Handlung durch das gesamte Ballett und ringen gegenüber dem Publikum um den letzten Stich.

Vladimir Malakhov hat sich immer besonders für die Rolle der Carabosse interessiert, weil sie in seinen Augen eine getanzte Charakterrolle ist. Auf den ersten Blick erscheint sie als Charakterrolle leicht zu besetzen, da sie technisch weniger virtuos disponiert wirkt, aber das Gegenteil ist der Fall. Die Rolle der Carabosse ist schwieriger als eine tänzerische Rolle, zumal sie die psychologisch differenzierteste Rolle des Balletts ist. Carabosse möchte ja der kleinen Aurora zur Taufe huldigen und sinnt erst auf Rache, als ihr dieser freundliche Akt verwehrt bleibt. Eine eindimensionale Darstellung und Choreografie würde der komplexen Anlage der Rolle nicht gerecht. Diese psychologischen Facetten sind es, die Malakhov interessieren. Er möchte nicht immer auf den Prinzen festgelegt sein und übernimmt daher selbst im Laufe der späteren Aufführungen in Berlin die Rolle der Carabosse. Ihn fasziniert es, als ein neuer Charakter auf die Bühne zu gehen, im Gegensatz zu anderen Tänzern, die Angst vor Charakterrollen haben und diese meiden, weil sie vermeintlich weniger publikumswirksam sind.

Malakhov benutzt die originalen französischen Namen der Feen, die als Patinnen zur Taufe Auroras eingeladen wurden. Da ist zum einen die Fee Canari qui chante, neben ihr folgen die Fee Candide, die Fee Fleur de farine, zudem die Fee Miettes qui tombent sowie die Fee Violante. Die Gaben der Feen können als Wunschvorstellungen und Erwartungen verstanden werden, die König und Königin für ihre Tochter Aurora erhoffen. Ihre Wünsche überreichen die guten Feen in Form von großen Fabergé-Eiern; eine Idee, die auf Malakhovs eigene Begeisterung für Fabergé-Eier zurück geht. Der Hof des Zaren hatte den Goldschmied Carl Fabergé 1885 damit beauftragt, ein Osterei besonderer Güte herzustellen. Fabergé entwarf ein aus Gold gefertigtes Ei, das kunstvoll mit Emaille überzogen war. Zar Alexander III. schenkte es seiner Gemahlin Maria Fjodorowna, und es wurde Tradition, dass der Zar seiner Familie zu Ostern Fabergé-Eier überreichte. Fabergé reüssierte und wurde zum Juwelier und Hofgoldschmied des Zaren berufen.

Die Feen bleiben in Malakhovs Version sichtbar, sie sind nicht wie üblich auf den Prolog beschränkt, sondern sie begleiten Aurora, nachdem sie sich gestochen hat und bewachen ihre Schlafstatt. Zu Beginn des zweiten Aktes treten sie noch einmal auf, sie übernehmen hier den Platz der Jagdgesellschaft aus der Urfassung. Dadurch bleibt der märchenhafte Charakter des Balletts ständig bestehen. Es sind die Feen, die die Geschicke der Personen lenken, allen voran die Fee Carabosse und die Fliederfee in ihrer Funktion als *Playmaker* des Balletts, die Handlung voranzutreiben. Zwei Dirigentinnen von Rang sozusagen.

Die zentrale Intention Malakhovs zielt primär auf die Erzählbarkeit des Märchens. Aus diesem Grund wird aus dem ursprünglichen Prolog und den drei Akten in der Produktion des Staatsballetts Berlin ein zweiaktiges Ballett. Um die strenge Ballettkonvention zugunsten der Erzählbarkeit des Märchens zu lösen, hat Vladimir Malakhov nur wenig in den Kanon eingegriffen. Die Hauptszenen des meisterlichen Balletts von Petipa bleiben unangetastet. Als ein Höhepunkt in *Dornröschen* erschienen bereits in der Urfassung von Petipa im Divertissement des dritten Aktes Zitate aus Perrault'schen Märchen. Divertissements sind kleine Ballette, die selbst ohne Handlung und ohne Bezug zur Haupthandlung aus selbständigen Tänzen bestehen und eine willkommene Gelegenheit für Virtuosität bieten. In *Dornröschen* sind das: Der gestiefelte Kater und die weiße Katze, Aschenbrödel und Prinz Fortuné, der Blaue Vogel und Prinzessin Florine, Rotkäppchen und der Wolf, sowie als letztes Klein Däumling und seine Brüder, bevor dann der Grand Pas de deux Aurora und Prinz Désiré virtuos vereint und im Tanzrausch über die Bühne geht. Da Malakhov das Ballett kürzen wollte, hat er den kleinen Däumling herausgenommen und das Rotkäppchen kommt ohne den Wolf, vielmehr trägt sie den Wolf um den Hals, der so nur als Anspielung erscheint. Um die Proportionen zu wahren, wurde der Blaue Vogel Pas de deux, einer der schwersten Pas de deux der Ballettliteratur überhaupt, leicht gekürzt.

Bühne und Kostüme im Rosengarten

Die Neuausrichtung des Balletts von Malakhov bedurfte einer adäquaten Umsetzung auch im Design von Bühnenausstattung und Kostümen. Der Aura des luftigen Rosengartens und der bunten Instrumentationspalette von Tschaikowskys Musik sollte adäquat entsprochen werden. Rosen und Dornen zierten die zauberhaften Figurinen von Valery Kungurov, der den dramaturgischen und inszenatorischen Vorstellungen Malakhovs visuellen Ausdruck verlieh. Eine kongeniale Zusammenarbeit. Dabei war es gar nicht einfach, zueinander zu finden. Vor Jahren schon einmal kam Kungurov mit seiner Zeichenmappe zu Malakhov und zeigte im Eilverfahren seine Arbeiten. Doch es war keine Zeit und kein Projekt in Aussicht, und die Mappe hatte Kungurov auch gleich wieder mitgenommen. Vor einem Jahr jedoch machte Kungurov Malakhov ein Geschenk: ein gerahmtes Bild von einer Figurine. Auf der Suche nach einem geeigneten Ausstatter für sein *Dornröschen* war sich Malakhov ganz sicher: Jener Russe hatte die nötige Phantasie, seine Ideen in Kostüme und Bühnenbild umzusetzen. Er musste nur noch gefunden werden. Ein Adresse oder Telefonnummer war nicht mehr vorhanden, nur der Eindruck schien bleibend, sonst erst einmal nichts. Glücklicherweise entdeckte Malakhov auf der Rückseite des Bildes das Etikett des Rahmenmachers. Ein Anruf war schnell getätigt und die Frage, ob dieser sich erinnern könne, wer die Rahmung des Bildes in Auftrag gegeben hatte, konnte positiv beschieden werden. Er hat sich erinnert, suchte noch einen Tag lang nach der Telefonnummer des Künstlers und von da ab ging alles ganz leicht. Valery Kungurov wohnte sogar unweit von Berlin, so dass nun zahlreiche Produktionsbesprechungen kurzfristig stattfinden konnten.

Die Vorstellung seiner Kostüm- und Bühnenbildentwürfe fand daraufhin vor den Mitarbeitern des Service der Stiftung Oper in Berlin statt: Vertreter aller drei Opernhäuser waren zugegen und rundum stellte sich große Begeisterung bei den Anwesenden über die Figurinen und Entwürfe ein. Die Freude über die Pracht und reiche Ausstattung gerade für dieses Ballett ließ jedoch unmittelbar nach dem ersten allgemeinen Entzücken die große Sorge aufkommen, ob der enorme Umfang der Produktion zeitgerecht umgesetzt werden könne. Es wurde kalkuliert und gerechnet, Stunden gezählt, abgeglichen und auf Machbarkeit hin überprüft. Es gab für das Staatsballett Berlin nur einen Ausweg und auch dies wiederum war eine gelungene Premiere für Berlin: Die zahlreichen Kostüme konnten nur so rechtzeitig fertig gestellt werden, indem in allen drei Kostümwerkstätten der Opernhäuser parallel genäht wurde. Hier sei an Rolf Liebermanns Wort im Rahmen seiner Berliner Lektionen erinnert, dass Berlin seiner Ansicht nach gar keine drei Opernhäuser brauche – sondern vier. Die Kostüme für die Komparserie wurden in der Komischen Oper gefertigt, die der Solisten wurden in der Staatsoper genäht und die Corps-de-Ballet-Kostüme in der Deutschen Oper Berlin. Diesem Haus an der Bismarckstrasse, zugleich Berlins größter Oper, wurde auch die Federführung angetragen, da die Produktion ja für die Bühne der Deutschen Oper Berlin bestimmt ist. Parallel zu den ersten Tanzproben der Solisten und der Choreografie der Feen wurden die Kostümanproben absolviert. Der erste Auftritt für die Tänzer in Kostüm und Maske wird wohl in lustiger, wenn auch arbeitsreicher Erinnerung bleiben. Groß war die Aufregung, als die Feen ihre Tütüs zu Gesicht bekamen. Die Teller haben einen solch enormen Durchmesser, dass die Tänzerinnen erst einige zusätzlichen Proben benötigten, um damit umgehen zu können, das Gleichgewicht zu halten und sich wie Feen zu bewegen lernen. Aber auch die Feenbegleiter sorgten für vergnügte Momente in der ganzen Compagnie, da sie pflichtbewusst ihrer Aufgabe als Partner nachkommen wollten, was wirklich nicht einfach war, weil sie den Feen nur noch mit ausgestreckten Armen entgegentreten konnten. Welche Fee möchte das schon? Groß war das Lachen und noch größer die Freude, als auch solche Probleme rasch gelöst werden konnten. Zur Einstudierung der Choreo-

Christiane Theobald und Frank Sistenich

grafie konnte Malakhov mit Valentina Savina als erster Ballett-
meisterin eine der versiertesten Expertinnen ihres Faches
weltweit gewinnen. In ihr vereinen sich gleich mehrere direkte
Traditionslinien zur Quelle des Werkes: Savina wurde noch von
Jelisaweta Gerdt unterrichtet, die ihrerseits Schülerin von Marius
Petipa, Enrico Cecchetti und Michail Fokin gewesen war.

Premiere in der Deutschen Oper Berlin

Die Premiere von Malakhovs *Dornröschen* fand am 26. Oktober
2005 statt. Rosenspaliere in der Deutschen Oper Berlin ge-
leiteten die Besucher zu den Foyers, und auch in den Treppen-
aufgängen folgten weitere wunderbare Gestecke und kündeten
von der Inszenierungsidee. Die Rosen weiteten auf diese Weise
den offenen Rosengarten der Bühne bis in die Zuschauerfoyers
aus. Ob in den Pausen oder der sich anschließenden Premieren-
feier: Die Gäste wurden selbst ein konstitutives Mitglied der
Inszenierung, sie wandelten durch den Pausen-Garten, und es
hatte den Anschein, als inspirierten Inszenierung, Kostüme und
Choreografie so manchen Besucher des Hauses, doch selbst
einmal Ausschau zu halten nach seiner Aurora oder ihrem
Prinzen Désiré.

Neben der kompositorischen Dichte und Genialität der
melodischen Einfälle, der höchst anspruchsvollen Choreografie
und beeindruckenden Umsetzung auf der Berliner Bühne
scheint es auch das Erlösungsversprechen der literarischen
Vorlage zu sein, das die Gäste immer wieder in den Armen von
Malakhovs *Dornröschen*-Aufführungen erwachen lässt. Es hat
den Anschein, dass in unser aller kollektivem Unbewussten bis
heute die Helden der Handlung als Projektionsflächen für unsere
eigenen Bedürfnisse dienen. Aurora und Prinz Désiré leben und
lieben uns vor, wonach wir uns sehnen. Sie sind für uns in ihrem
Fühlen und Handeln real und fiktiv zugleich. Real sind sie, da
auch wir die widrigen Umstände unseres Lebens aus eigenem
Erleben nur zu gut kennen und nach Erlösung oder Befreiung
suchen. Fiktiv erscheinen sie uns, da das Happy End im realen
Leben oft noch aussteht und länger als uns lieb ist, auf sich
warten lässt. Die guten und die bösen Mächte in den aufge-
werteten Rollen der Fliederfee und der Fee Carabosse gehören
also zusammen, sie bedingen sich und werden in der Berliner
Dornröschen-Produktion durch das Symbol der Rose verbunden.
Die Rose mit ihrer schönen Blüte und den gefährlichen Dornen
als historisches Blumensymbol der Verständigung und der
Versöhnung dient als Mittlerin zwischen diesen beiden Welten,
ohne die es kein glückliches Ende gäbe. Und wenn dem so ist,
hat sich seit der Uraufführung am 3. Januar 1890 bis zur aktuel-
len Berliner Premiere kaum etwas geändert und wir dürfen
die These wagen, *Dornröschen* war, ist und bleibt in der Gunst
seines Publikums auf ewig unsterblich.

Christiane Theobald und Frank Sistenich

Malakhov's *Sleeping Beauty* for the Berlin State Ballet

The Sleeping Beauty, a story of success

The wish to think in superlatives does not seem to be a child of our time a one. Even Tchaikovsky reportedly favoured *The Sleeping Beauty* as his best and and most accomplished ballet. This work was the pride of his oeuvre, a sparkle of elaborately cut gems. Now it is up to the choreographers and dancers of our time to attend to this treasure, polish and present it to the audience in its most beautiful form again and again. Composers, generations of dancers and the audience too are in unanimous agreement that Tchaikovsky's *Sleeping Beauty* is one of the most beautiful and magnificent ballets in dance literature. Wherever else do we find such a unanimous response in the world of great art? Of Igor Stravinsky we know that he said: "I have just read again the score of this ballet. (…) I have spend some days of intense pleasure in finding therein again and again the same feeling of freshness, inventiveness, ingenuity, and vigour. And I warmly desire that your audiences of all countries may feel this work as it is felt by me, a Russian musician." And Rudolf Nureyev once stated: "*The Sleeping Beauty* is the ballet of ballets. My first teacher always called it the queen of the ballets." Until our day, the audience has known about the fundamental effect of this classic.

As comprehensive as the story of success of *The Sleeping Beauty* may seem today, at first it did not look as if this ballet would be the key work and quintessence of Tchaikovsky's œuvre. His first major ballet music, *Swan Lake*, had been written as early as 1875/76, but the ballet unfortunately was not blessed with immediate, resounding success after the first performances in Moscow. *Swan Lake* was regarded as an unpretentious work with old stage designs and costumes which had been put together for the occasion. Although the music already showed the exceptionally gifted symphonist, unusual for the genre of the classical ballet, Tchaikovsky had shelved the subject of ballet music; he withdrew and devoted himself to other music genres. In May 1888, however, Ivan A. Vsevolozhsky, the outstanding theatre director of the Imperial Theatres of St. Petersburg, who had recognized the talent of Tchaikovsky very early, had "been thinking of writing a libretto on Perrault's fairy tale *La belle au bois dormant* … I want to stage it in the style of Louis XIV. … In the last act there needs to be a quadrille made from all Perrault's fairy stories." (quoted from a letter of Vsevolozhsky dated 13 May 1888 to Tchaikovsky). The idea for the ballet of *The Sleeping Beauty* was born. Its great success is largely due to Vsevolozhsky and his great interest in ballets. As theatre director, he was well aware of what this art form required. His commitment to Tchaikovsky's stage works was boundless, and he must also have been an interesting man, with a sharp mind, style and sophistication. Tchaikovsky liked all of that, and this was the prerequisite for the wonderful collaboration between Vsevolozhsky, Tchaikovsky and Petipa which led to the first magnificent production of *The Sleeping Beauty*. Committing himself wholeheartedly to this project, Vsevolozhsky alone delivered 221 custom designs for the ballet. It was the stylistic possibilities of the project thanks to the combination of these three protagonists that quickly convinced the composer. In August of the same year Tchaikovsky already received the libretto from his theatre director and was "charmed, delighted beyond all description". It fitted in perfectly with the tradition of ballet fairy tales which were very popular in Russia at that time.

Vsevolozhsky adapted Perrault's story, met the demands of the tsarist court for pompous entertainment and did not forget to offer to the Tsar the subliminally expected flattery. The story was now an abridged and revised version of the folk tale, a story in the framework of which the art of classical ballet, presented in various large divertissements, could develop with all its possibilities. On 25 July 1889, while working on the orchestration of the score, Tchaikovsky wrote to Mrs von Meck: "The subject is so poetic, musically so grateful, that I was completely carried away in composing it".

The libretto is written in such a way that the audience already knows at the end of the prologue how the story will turn out. Spectacular dance scenes as compensation for a less important story are characteristic of ballet fairy plays, and this is why today everyone thinks of wonderful music and a magnificent choreography in connection with *The Sleeping Beauty*. "If the dramatic structure of *The Sleeping Beauty* is judged by the requirements of the dramatic theatre, it seems feeble and extremely long-winded. Even for an opera, it would be monotonous and boring. But as the principles of the symphonic development of the action are observed, it is an almost ideal basis for a ballet." (Vera Krasovskaya, Dornröschen – ein Schlüsselwerk der Ballettgeschichte). Tchaikovsky himself once remarked that going to a ballet mainly because of the story was akin to the wish to go to an opera because of the recitatives. For Tchaikovsky, the composer, the form of *The Sleeping Beauty* as his best ballet was closer to the symphony than to the drama, and as regards the choreographer Marius Petipa, *The Sleeping Beauty* was his opus magnum as well. "The Sleeping Beauty is the strongest and most perfect ballet of Petipa, practically summing up the choreographer's long, difficult and persistent search for the synthesis of symphony and ballet." (Vera Krasovskaya). Petipa followed the prevailing principles of construction by dividing the ballet into a conventional pantomime to make the story clear on the one hand, and into a classical dance to express the emotions on the other. At over 70 years of age, the choreographer delivered his masterpiece, thus crowning not only his own artistic œuvre. Petipa's *Sleeping Beauty* becomes the epitome of the style of a whole epoch, of performances "à grand ballet". Until that moment on 3 January 1890, the world had never seen a more perfect ballet. "It seems to me that it has created a harmony, a harmony, unique in its kind, between the choreographer, the composer, the stage designer and the performers (…). This is also Tchaikovsky's most perfect, most choreography-related ballet. The music is characterized by an inexplicable warmth and cheerfulness, by a very special tonal harmony which, nowhere repeated, leads us into an amazing, fabulous world." (Leonid V. Jacobson, Petipas Geheimnis).

The music of Peter I. Tchaikovsky

When Peter I. Tchaikovsky later calculated the time he had actually spent on composing this work, apart from the orchestration, he found that he had written these wonderful three hours of music in only forty days. On the last page of the particell Tchaikovsky wrote: "I finished the sketches on 7 June 1889 at 8 p.m. … Praise be to God! In all I worked ten days in October, three weeks in January, and now a week!" Tchaikovsky seemed to have been extremely motivated, probably also due to the lucky combination of these three protagonists who were mainly responsible for this project. On 13 August he wrote again to his friend and patroness: "I have engaged in scoring it with special love and care, and I have devised several completely new orchestral combinations which I hope will be very beautiful and interesting." Tchaikovsky ignited a genuine fireworks of light sparkling colours within a meticulously composed dance programme. The composer put Petipa's scenario in music, converted the dramatic development of the story into musical action, and created an excellent balance between pantomime and classical dance in close agreement with the choreographer Petipa. "Before he started work, he asked the ballet master Marius Petipa to describe in minute detail the dances, the number of bars, the type of music, the bar length of each number." (Modest Tchaikovsky: Das Leben Peter I. Tschaikowskys).

In his ballet *Swan Lake*, Tchaikovsky had already used leitmotifs, assigning them to the central characters of the work. In the case of *The Sleeping Beauty*, the composer picked up the thread of the leitmovic work again and conceived both the musical and the dramatic main characters of the ballet: It is not Aurora or Prince Désiré who are the focus of acoustic attention,

but the good Lilac Fairy and the evil fairy Carabosse. Both fairies are accompanied by their leitmotifs when they make their entrance on the stage or in order to announce their intentions in the musical action. "Although Princess Aurora and Prince Désiré are regarded as main characters in *The Sleeping Beauty* and they of all characters have been provided with a wealth of classical dance scenes, the fairy Carabosse and the Lilac Fairy remain the central story-moving characters. And while the Lilac Fairy is sketched as a very simple character (…), the fairy Carabosse, a dancing and pantomimic character, is perfect." (Leonid W. Jakobson, Pepitas Geheimnis). This structure has been adopted by Vladimir Malakhov as well, by bringing both fairies to the centre of the story in his choreography.

Among the most ardent admirers of the works by Petipa was Michael Fokin who choreographed Diaghilev's Ballets Russes. In the first two decades of the 20th century, Russian dancers again and again performed extracts from *The Sleeping Beauty* outside Russia but the first memorable production beyond the borders of Russia was staged in London in 1921 as *The Sleeping Princess* with Diaghilev's Ballets Russes. The fabulous scenery and costumes at that time were by Léon Bakst. On 18 October Igor Stravinsky who had participated in the musical preparation wrote his famous open letter to Serge Diaghilev in *The Times* which concluded with the words: "I am very glad that I was able to participate in this performance for I like Tchaikovsky; but I also admire the classical ballet, the beauty of its order and the aristocratic strictness of its form. His attitude conforms exactly with the view I have of art. In the classical dance I see the triumph of moderate planning over wandering feelings, of rule over arbitrariness, of order over 'chance'."

Tchaikovsky was a reformer of ballet music, freeing the ballet from the hands of a Ludwig Minkus and transferring his symphonic demands to the composition for the ballet, an impulse that was further developed by Igor Stravinsky later. Rhythm, orchestration and tonal structure were treated by Tchaikovsky to a new level. His ballet music shows how he knew how to balance the needs of the choreographer with his own needs as a composer. All of a sudden, ballet music was basically more symphonic. On 28 February 1889 Tchaikovsky wrote his publisher P. I. Jurgenson: "The ballet certainly is akin to the symphony." Tchaikovsky performed the most progressive synthesis of symphony and ballet music ever produced until that time. The often cited allegation that Tchaikovsky's music was sweet amounts to nothing, shedding light on the subjective disposition of the audience rather than on the objective quality of the composition itself. In this context, one should mention a bon mot by Sergiu Celibidache about Rimsky-Korsakov who once remarked that whoever thinks this music is too sweet always brings his diabetes with him to the performance. "Tchaikovsky's music is wonderful, and the whole fairy tale is contained therein. Dancers love Tchaikovsky for it, the only thing they have to do is to dance." (Vladimir Malakhov).

Tchaikovsky's authority even made the choreographer Marius Petipa truly work together with him. "Petipa respected Tchaikovsky to the highest, and if he did not fear him, he appreciated the collaboration with him. In view of the ambitious goal, every detail was important. Of course, Petipa did not demand of Tchaikovsky the same as he would have of less important composers, but whatever Tchaikovsky could give him was taken by the ballet master with his usual energy." (Vera Krasovskaya, Dornröschen – ein Schlüsselwerk der Ballettgeschichte). The collaboration between the two artists in the heyday of the development of the ballet was exemplary and completely synergetic. Even if the historical sources of their contemporaries are not always in agreement as to the smoothness of the collaboration between the two artists, they document at least a stroke of luck for the ballet repertoire, such as later achieved only between Stravinsky and various choreographers. The extremely broad range of orchestration, the well-balanced structure of scenes, dances and divertissements, the variety of forms, and the wealth of musical ideas in comparison with quality and quantity have never again been achieved until this day. "The Russian style of the music so powerfully represented by Tchaikovsky in the past years is noticeable time and again. The music so perfectly matches the costumes and the character of the work, having a tinge of Frenchness in it, yet tasting Russian at the same time. Whatever others may feel, I am deeply in love with this French story which is accompanied by Russian music." (Herrman A. Laroche, Peter I. Tschaikowsky).

Malakhov's version for Berlin and the central role of the fairies

Vladimir Malakhov is in the direct tradition of the authors of the ballet fairy tale *The Sleeping Beauty*: Petipa and Tchaikovsky. Since his education and training in Moscow, he has grown up with Tchaikovsky and *The Sleeping Beauty*, having danced the role of Prince Désiré far more than 100 times in various productions all over the world. Even his Berlin premiere as a dancer was under the star of this magnificent ballet. In 1995 he danced Prince Désiré in the legendary version of Rudolf Nureyev on the stage of the Berlin State Opera Unter den Linden. Since that time, he had been a regular guest performer in Berlin until he was persuaded in 2002 to assume the artistic direction of the ballet of the Berlin State Opera and eventually, since 2004, control the fortunes of the largest ballet ensemble of Germany, consisting of 88 dancers, as director of the Berlin State Opera.

The world of tales and images of the strikingly French ballet fairy tale has always intrigued Malakhov, and hence, it is not surprising that he intended to produce his own version of the "ballet of ballets". He reduced the extremely long work to about two hours, supported by Alexander Sotnikov who also acted as musical director of the production. A true expert on the ballet scores of Tchaikovsky, Sotnikov has performed many different versions of *The Sleeping Beauty* and is an experienced adviser on every abridgement and modification of the score. In contrast to the classical version, Malakhov changed the setting by adapting it more to the congenial music of Tchaikovsky. The transformation of the story into a blossoming rose garden now matches ideally with the very colourful orchestration of the score. The fairy tale is no longer set in an old castle but virtually in the open in the midst of Mother Nature. It is a magic garden, a *hortus conclusus*, surrounded only by rose bushes and rose hedges. Malakhov is a passionate lover of flowers. "Roses create the atmosphere in my *Sleeping Beauty*. They are virtually everywhere. And throughout the evening their number even increases, for the rose hedge grows higher in each act. One has to see how they smell." The roses have flowers and thorns. The good world and the evil world collide even through the stage design. The thorns of the rose symbolize pain but also fear. The thorn hedge behind which the Sleeping Beauty has been sleeping for hundred years is a symbol of protection on the one hand and of separation and hope for salvation on the other.

The central accent of the ballet in Malakhov's version is the role of the Lilac Fairy. In Nureyev's version of *The Sleeping Beauty*, this part is still a stepping dance role. In the Berlin production of Malakhov, the Lilac Fairy is almost always present on the stage, toe dancing and performing wonderful variations to the music which, in the original version, have been reserved to the solo of the prince. A real treat for every dancer of this role who has always dreamt of dancing to this music one day. The good Lilac Fairy has internalized the qualities of humility and charity. No happy ending and no salvation would be possible without her. It will be up to her to guide the intrepid prince to the Sleeping Beauty.

The adversary of the good Lilac Fairy, the evil fairy Carabosse (danced by a man in the original version already), embodies the dark sides of life. Since the king forgot to invite the fairy Carabosse to the christening of Princess Aurora, unlike many other fairies who bestow their blessings on the infant, she curses the newly born: Aurora will one day prick her finger and die.

But the intervention of the good Lilac Fairy moderates the curse on Aurora. The pricking of the finger – on the Berlin stage by a poisoned rose, not by a spindle as in the original – will be followed by a deep sleep of hundred years behind a thorn hedge, and only the kiss of a prince who succeeds to get through the thorn hedge can awaken the sleeping Aurora. The remarkable thing about the Berlin production of *The Sleeping Beauty* is that this role, too, is given greater significance by Malakhov, compared to the original version. Carabosse takes part in the final tableau, appearing on stage at the wedding and holding up the flow of the happy-ending story. The general rest in the last scene and the attention of both the audience and the performers are focussed on her. She is out for revenge, and good and evil, characterized by the fairy Carabosse and the Lilac Fairy, collide again. They compete with each other until the coda, not only leitmotivically in the orchestral pit but also through their dance on the stage. They control and guide the story through the whole ballet and, facing the audience, struggle for the last trick.

Vladimir Malakhov has always had a special interest in the role of Carabosse because, in his eyes, it is a danced character role. At first glance, it appears easy to cast since it seems to be technically less virtuoso but the exact opposite is true. The role of Carabosse is more difficult than a dance role, particularly since it is, psychologically, the most complex role of the ballet. Carabosse originally wants to bestow blessings on little Aurora and only is out for revenge when she is kept from performing this friendly act. A one-dimensional presentation and choreography would not do justice to the complexity of the role. It is these psychological factors which Malakhov is interested in. Not wanting to always play the prince, he plays the role of Carabosse himself in later performances in Berlin. It fascinates him to enter the stage as a new character – unlike other dancers who are afraid of character roles and avoid them because they are supposed to have less public appeal.

Malakhov uses the original French names of the fairies who were invited to the christening of Aurora as godmothers. There is, on the one hand, the fairy Canari qui chante. The other fairies are Candide, the fairy Fleur de farine, the fairy Miettes qui tombent and the fairy Violante. The presents of the fairies can be understood as wishful thinking and expectations of the king and the queen for their daughter Aurora. The good fairies bestow their wishes in the form of large Fabergé eggs; this idea goes back to Malakhov's own enthusiasm for Fabergé eggs. In 1885, the court of the Tsar commissioned the goldsmith Carl Fabergé to create a special Easter egg of exceptional quality. Fabergé created a golden egg elaborately covered with enamel which Tsar Alexander III gave to his wife Maria Feodorovna as a present. Henceforth, it became a tradition that the Tsar presented his family Fabergé eggs at Easter. Fabergé was successful and was appointed jeweler and goldsmith to the court of the Tsar. The fairies remain visible in Malakhov's version, their appearance is not as usual limited to the prologue. Instead, they accompany Aurora after she had pricked her finger, and guard her slumber. At the beginning of the second act, they appear again, taking the place of the hunting party from the original version. Thus, the fairy-like character of the ballet remains for it is the fairies who control the fate of the characters – first and foremost the fairy Carabosse and the Lilac Fairy in their function as playmakers of the ballet to push the story ahead. Two first-class conductors, so to speak.

Malakhov's central intention aims primarily at the tellability of the fairy tale. For this reason, the original prologue and the three acts are turned into a two-act ballet in the production of the Berlin State Ballet. In order to undo the rigid ballet conventions in favour of the tellability of the fairy tale, Vladimir Malakhov intervened only a little in the canon. The main scenes of the masterly ballet by Petipa have remained unaffected. As a highlight in *The Sleeping Beauty*, the original version of Petipa already contained quotes from Perrault's fairy tales in the divertissement of the third act. Divertissements are little ballets consisting of independent dances, even without a story and without any connection with the main action, and offering a welcome opportunity for virtuosity. In *The Sleeping Beauty* these are: Puss in Boots and the White Cat, Cinderella and Prince Fortuné, the Bluebird and Princess Florine, Little Red Riding Hood and the Wolf, and Tom Thumb and his brothers before the Grand Pas de Deux unites Aurora and Prince Desiré in a virtuoso manner and is performed in a dancing frenzy.

Since Malakhov wanted to shorten the ballet, he removed Tom Thumb, and Little Red Riding Hood appears without the wolf who is only alluded to her by having the wolf around her neck. In order to preserve the proportions, the pas de deux of the Bluebird, one of the most difficult pas de deux in ballet literature, was slightly shortened.

Scenery and costumes in the rose garden

The reorientation of Malakhov's ballet required its adequate realization even in the design of the stage set and the costumes. The aura of the airy rose garden and the colourful range of orchestration of Tchaikovsky's music were to be reflected therein. Roses and thorns adorned the charming costume designs by Valery Kungurov who gave visual expression to the dramatic and staging ideas of Malakhov. A congenial collaboration! Even though it was not easy for them to find each other. Some years before, Kungurov had come to Malakhov and showed him some of his drawings in a rush. But at that time, time was non-existent and no project was in prospect so that Kungurov took his portfolio right back with him. A year ago, however, Kungurov sent Malakhov a present: a framed picture of a costume design. Looking for the right designer for his *Sleeping Beauty*, Malakhov was sure that that Russian possessed the necessary imagination to incorporate his ideas into the costumes and the décor. He just had to be found. An address or telephone number did not exist, only the impression he had made seemed to remain – nothing else. Fortunately, Malakhov discovered the label of the frame-maker on the back of the picture who was called at once and answered the question as to whether he was able to remember the person who had ordered the framing of the picture in the affirmative. He remembered the artist, looked for his telephone number for a whole day, and then everything was very easy. It turned out that Valery Kungurov lived not far from Berlin so that many production meetings could take place at short notice.

The presentation of his costume and stage set designs took place in the presence of the service staff of the "Stiftung Oper in Berlin": representatives of all three opera houses were present, and everyone was very enthusiastic about the costume and stage set designs. When the first pleasing excitement was over, however, their enjoyment of the splendour and lavish décor especially for this ballet was soon marred by the worry about whether the enormous scope of the production could be realized in time. They calculated and estimated, counted hours and examined the production for feasibility. There was only one way out for the Berlin State Ballet, and even that was a successful début for Berlin: The numerous costumes could only be completed in time if the wardrobes of all three opera houses sewed the costumes simultaneously. This brings to mind a remark of Rolf Liebermann at his "Berliner Lektionen" that, in his opinion, Berlin does not need three opera houses – but four. The costumes of the supernumeraries were completed at the Komische Oper, the costumes of the soloists at the State Opera, and the costumes of the corps de ballet at the Berlin Deutsche Oper. The latter opera house, the largest opera of Berlin located at the Bismarckstrasse, was in overall control of the project since the production was designed for the stage of the Berlin Deutsche Oper. The costume fittings were held at the same time as the first dance rehearsals of the soloists and the choreography of the fairies. Everyone will probably have funny, yet busy memories of the dancers' first appearance in costumes and masks. When the fairies set eyes on their tutus, everybody was in a flurry of excitement. The diameter of the plates was so large that the dancers needed extra rehearsals in order to learn how to keep their balance and how to move like fairies. But the dance partners of the fairies also caused some funny moments in the whole company when they dutifully wanted to perform their task as partners, which proved to be quite difficult because they could only advance towards the fairies with outstretched arms. Which fairy would want that? The laughter was hilarious, yet the joy was even greater when such problems could be solved quickly. Malakhov had succeeded in winning Valentina Savina, one of the most versed experts of her trade throughout the world, as first ballet mistress for the rehearsals of the ballet choreography. In her, several direct lines of tradition with regard to the source of the work are united: Savina was taught by Yelisaveta Gerdt who, in turn, had been a pupil of Marius Petipa, Enrico Cecchetti and Michail Fokin.

Premiere at the Berlin Deutsche Oper

The premiere of Malakhov's *Sleeping Beauty* took place on 26 October 2005. Trellises of roses in the Berlin Deutsche Oper showed the visitors the way to the foyers, and even the stairways were adorned by beautiful flower arrangements, hinting at the idea of the production. These roses expand the open rose garden of the stage to the public foyers. Whether in the intermissions or at the subsequent premiere party: The guests themselves became constitutive members of the production, strolling through the intermission garden, and it appeared as if the production, costumes and choreography had inspired many a visitor of the theatre to look for his own Aurora or her own Prince Désiré.

Apart from the compositional density and ingenuity of the melodic ideas, the highly demanding choreography and the impressing realization on the stage in Berlin, it is also the promise of salvation of the literary original that seems to make the guests awaken again and again in the arms of Malakhov's performances of *The Sleeping Beauty*. It appears as if until today the heroes of the story serve as projection areas for our own needs in our collective unconscious. Aurora and Prince Désiré set an example in the way they love and live which we are longing for. In their feelings and actions they are real, yet at the same time fictitious to us. They are real to us because we, too, knowing unfavourable circumstances in our lives quite well from personal experience, are looking for salvation or liberation. They seem fictitious to us because the happy ending often is still to come in real life, taking too much time for our liking. The good and the evil powers in the enhanced roles of the Lilac Fairy and the fairy

Carabosse belong together, they are interdependent and, in the Berlin production of *The Sleeping Beauty*, are united by the symbol of the rose. The rose with its beautiful flower and dangerous thorns as historical flower symbol of understanding and reconciliation serves as a mediator between these two worlds; without it, there would be no happy ending. And if that is the case, there has been hardly any change since the world premiere on 3 January 1890 until the current premiere in Berlin, and we may dare make the case that the *Sleeping Beauty* was, is and will forever be immortal and in the good graces of her audience.

Christiane Theobald and Frank Sistenich

Die Besetzung · The cast

Ballett in drei Akten mit Prolog
Musik Peter I. Tschaikowsky
Choreographie und Inszenierung Vladimir Malakhov nach Marius Petipa
Bühnenbild und Kostüme Valery Kungurov
Licht Andrey Tarassov
Premiere am 26. Oktober 2005 in der Deutschen Oper Berlin

Musikalische Leitung Alexander Sotnikov
Orchester der Deutschen Oper Berlin

Prinzessin Aurora **Diana Vishneva*** | Polina Semionova | Nadja Saidakova | Corinne Verdeil
Prinz Désiré **Vladimir Malakhov** | Artem Shpilevsky | Ronald Savkovic
Fée des Lilas **Beatrice Knop** | Maria Seletskaja | Viara Natcheva
Carabosse **Michael Banzhaf** | Vladimir Malakhov | Ronald Savkovic
König Florestan XIV. **Alexander Chmelnitzky**
Die Königin **Birgit Brux** | Kathlyn Pope | Barbara Schroeder
Catalabutte, der Zeremonienmeister **Oliver Wulff**

Prolog
(Catalabutte, der König, die Königin, Fée des Lilas, Carabosse)
Die Feen
Candide **Elena Pris**
Fleur de farine **Gaela Pujol** | Nadia Yanowsky
Miettes qui tombent **Sebnem Gülseker**
Canari qui chante **Iana Salenko** | Alessandra Pasquali
Violante **Corinne Verdeil** | Maria-Helena Buckley
Ihre Begleiter Christian Krehl | Artur Lill | Sven Seidelmann
Martin Szymanski | Dinu Tamzlacaru | Robert Wohlert
Begleiter der Carabosse Dmitri Boulgakov | Marian Lazar
Yann Vandenhaute | Mario Hernandez | Ulian Topor

Erster Akt
(Prinzessin Aurora, der König, die Königin, Catalabutte, Fée des Lilas, die anderen Feen, Carabosse, ihre Begleiter)
Auroras Freundinnen Emi Hariyama | Johanna Hwang
Alessandra Pasquali | Nadia Yanowsky | Sarah Mestrovic
Brenda Saleh | Barbara Schroeder | Nanami Terai
Vier Prinzen **Martin Buczkó** | **Wieslaw Dudek** | **Leonard Jakovina** | **Ibrahim Önal** | Arshak Ghalumyan | Martin Szymanski

Zweiter Akt
(Prinz Désiré, Fée des Lilas, die anderen Feen, Carabosse, ihre Begleiter, das ›Traumbild‹ von Prinzessin Aurora)

Dritter Akt
(Prinzessin Aurora, Prinz Désiré, der König, die Königin, Catalabutte, Fée des Lilas, die anderen Feen, Carabosse)
Die Edelsteine
Rubin **Maria-Helena Buckley** | Gaela Pujol
Smaragd **Nanami Terai**
Saphir **Stephanie Greenwald**
Diamant **Viara Natcheva** | Maria Seletskaja
Cinderella und Prinz Fortuné **Alessandra Pasquali – Leonard Jakovina** | Natalia Munoz – Sven Seidelmann/Rainer Krenstetter
Prinzessin Florine und der Blaue Vogel **Nadia Yanowsky – Rainer Krenstetter** | Iana Salenko – Marian Walter/Dinu Tamazlacaru
Kater und Kätzchen **Johanna Hwang – Artur Lill** | Maria Giambona – Javier Peña Vazquez/Vladislav Marinov
Rotkäppchen **Iana Balova** | Quinn Pendleton
sowie Solisten und Corps de ballet des Staatsballetts Berlin

Intendant Vladimir Malakhov
Geschäftsführender Direktor Georg Vierthaler
Stellvertretende Intendantin und Betriebsdirektorin
Dr. Christiane Theobald
Produktionsleitung Charlotte Butler
Erste Ballettmeisterin Valentina Savina
Ballettmeister Christine Camillo | Alexander Chmelnitzky
Tomas Karlborg | Andrej Klemm | Monika Lubitz
Choreologie Marzena Sobanska | Korina Stolz-Franke
Pianisten Peter Hartwig | Nodira Burkhanova | Marita Mirsalimova | Klaus Pippig

* Premierenbesetzung hervorgehoben

Die Handlung

Prolog
(Ein königlicher Garten)

Dem König Florestan XIV. und seiner Königin ist ihr sehnlichster Wunsch erfüllt worden: die Königin hat eine Prinzessin zur Welt gebracht und ihr den Namen Aurora, die Morgenröte, gegeben. Es wird ein großes Fest gefeiert. Sechs Feen erscheinen, um der neugeborenen Prinzessin ihre Segenswünsche auf den Weg ins Leben mitzugeben. Verspätet erscheint schließlich die böse Fee Carabosse, die der Hofzeremonienmeister Catalabutte einzuladen vergaß. Sie wünscht der Prinzessin einen frühen Tod. Die Fliederfee kann diese Verwünschung nur noch in einen hundertjährigen Schlaf verwandeln.

Erster Akt

Die herangewachsene Prinzessin feiert Geburtstag. Von ihren Eltern sind auch vier Prinzen geladen, die um die Hand Auroras anhalten. Sie weist sie aber alle ab. Die böse Fee Carabosse nähert sich der Prinzessin und schenkt ihr eine der schönsten und verführerischsten Rosen, die sie je gesehen hat. Aurora sticht sich an den Dornen und verfällt sogleich dem bösen Zauber. Die Fliederfee erfüllt ihre Verheißung und wandelt, wie sie es versprochen hatte, den Tod in einen hundertjährigen Schlaf, in den der ganze Hofstaat versinkt, beschützt von einer undurchdringlichen, dornigen Rosenhecke.

Zweiter Akt

Als hundert Jahre vergangen sind, sucht die Fliederfee einen jungen Prinzen, der Aurora erlösen könnte. Sie findet ihn in Désiré, dem sie in einem zauberischen Waldstück begegnet, wo die Feen ihr fröhliches Unwesen mit ihm treiben. Sie lässt vor ihm Prinzessin Aurora erscheinen. In Liebe entbrannt folgt Désiré der Fliederfee und kann durch die Dornenhecke bis zur schlafenden Prinzessin vordringen. Sein Kuss löst den Bann, und mit der Prinzessin erwacht das Leben wieder.

Dritter Akt

Der König lässt zur Hochzeit von Aurora und Désiré einen großen Ball ausrichten. In strahlenden Divertissements wird dem Hochzeitspaar gehuldigt, es tanzen Edelsteine und Märchenfiguren. Apotheose.

The plot

Prolog
(A royal garden)

King Florestan XIV. and his Queen's fondest wish has been fulfilled: The Queen gave birth to a princess and named her Aurora, the dawn. In compliment to her there will be celebrated a grand feast. Six fairies appear to give Aurora all of their blessings on her way to life. Fairy Carabosse eventually appears late, though the master of ceremonies forgot to invite her. Carabosse's gift to Aurora is a curse: her early dead should approach the princess soon. Fortunately the Lilac Fairy promises to convert this ban on Aurora into a deep sleep for a hundred years.

First Act

The grown up princess celebrates her birthday. Her parents invited four princes, who ask for Aurora's hand – but she refuses to all of them. Carabosse approaches her, and gives her as a present one of the most beautiful and tempting roses Aurora has ever seen. But she pricks her finger on a thorn and falls into a deep stiffness. The Lilac Fairy though, as she has promised turns her death into the sleep of a hundred years in which not only the princess falls but the whole royal court. All of them were protected by an enormous, impenetrable, thorny rosehedge.

Second Act

When the hundred years have passed, the Lilac Fairy seeks for a young prince to release Aurora from her ban. She finds that person in Désiré, who she encounters in a bewitched part of the forest, where the fairies play their joyous mischief with him. The Lilac Fairy conjures up a vision of Aurora. Being aroused with love Désiré follows the fairy through the rosehedge to the sleeping princess. His kiss releases the ban and with the princesses' awakening the whole court starts to come back to life.

Third Act

The King stages a big wedding feast for Princess Aurora and Prince Désiré. In the brightest divertissement the court renders their homage to the bridal pair – gemstones and fairy tale figures dance. Apotheose.

Akt 1

10.15 Uhr, vor dem Training

1 Sergej Upkin
2 Polina Semionova
3 Sergej Upkin (vorne), Christian
Krehl und Vladislav Marinov
4 Xenia Wiest, Quinn Pendleton
5 Vladislav Marinov
6 Robert Wohlert, Artur Lill, Michael
Banzhaf und Marian Walter
7 Leonard Jakovina und
Vladimir Malakhov

10.15 a.m., before the class

1 Sergej Upkin
2 Polina Semionova
3 Sergej Upkin (in front), Christian
Krehl and Vladislav Marinov
4 Xenia Wiest, Quinn Pendleton
5 Vladislav Marinov
6 Robert Wohlert, Artur Lill, Michael
Banzhaf und Marian Walter
7 Leonard Jakovina and
Vladimir Malakhov

Akt 1 **27**

90 Minuten Trainingspflicht am
Vormittag. Die Kür folgt am Abend

1 Polina Semionova, Uliana Selezkaja
 (links)
2 Andrej Klemm, Leonard Jakovina und
 Elena Pris (von vorne nach hinten)
3 Steffen Neumann und Sven
 Seidelmann (von vorne nach hinten)
4 Maria Giambona, Shirin Nazimov
 und Leonard Jakovina (von vorne
 nach hinten)
5 Bettina Thiel, Aymeric Mosselmans
 und Christian Krehl
6 Elodie Estève

90 minutes compulsory exercises
in the morning, followed by the
performance in the evening

1 Polina Semionova, Uliana Selezkaja
 (left)
2 Andrej Klemm, Leonard Jakovina
 and Elena Pris (from front to back)
3 Steffen Neumann and Sven
 Seidelmann (from front to back)
4 Maria Giambona, Shirin Nazimov
 and Leonard Jakovina (from front
 to back)
5 Bettina Thiel, Aymeric Mosselmans
 and Christian Krehl
6 Elodie Estève

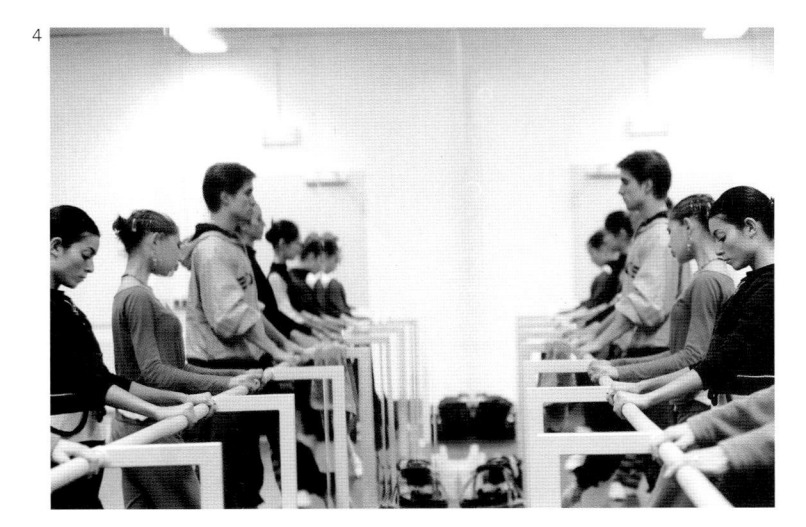

Akt 1 **29**

Vladimir Malakhov – der Intendant als Primus inter pares

1/2 Vladimir Malakhov
 3 Mit Alessandra Pasquali, Nadia Yanowsky, Emi Hariyama und Johanna Hwang (von links nach rechts)
 4 Vladimir Malakhov
 5 Mit Arshak Ghalumyan, Andrej Klemm und Birgit Brux (von links nach rechts)

Vladimir Malakhov – the director as primus inter pares

1/2 Vladimir Malakhov
 3 With Alessandra Pasquali, Nadia Yanowsky, Emi Hariyama and Johanna Hwang (from left to right)
 4 Vladimir Malakhov
 5 With Arshak Ghalumyan, Andrej Klemm and Birgit Brux (from left to right)

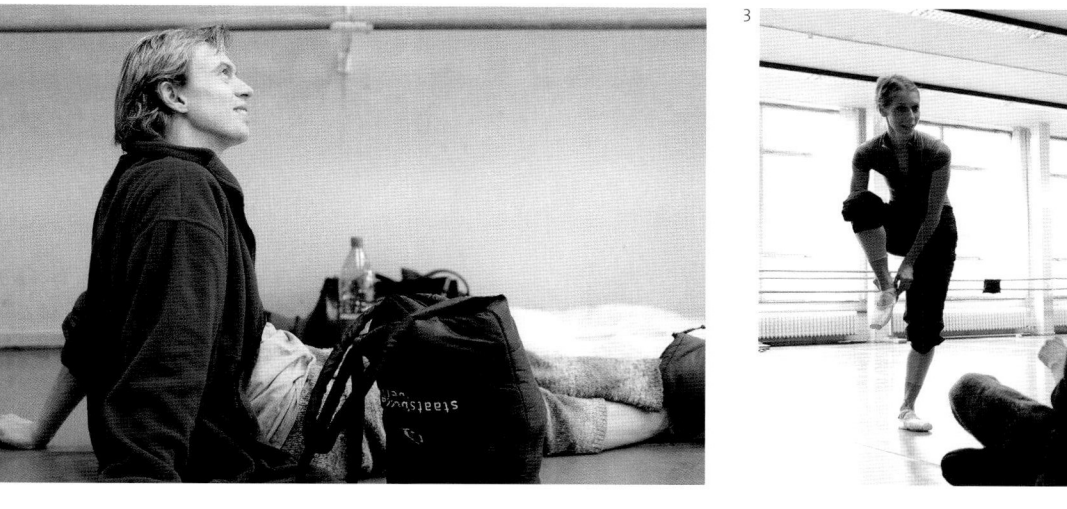

Akt 1 **31**

Zwischen Training und Vorstellung: private ›Ansichten‹ der Solisten

Barbara Schroeder

1 Beim Training
2 Mit Nadja Saidakova und Vladimir Malakhov
3 Mit Martin Szymanski und Julius

Viara Natcheva

4/5 Viara Natcheva
6 Zur Abwechslung Schwanensee

Between training and performance: private "views" of the soloists

Barbara Schroeder

1 In class
2 With Nadja Saidakova and Vladimir Malakhov
3 With Martin Szymanski and Julius

Viara Natcheva

4/5 Viara Natcheva
6 Swan lake, for a change

Training für die Fée Violante – Corinne Verdeil

1 Frisch vom Friseur
2 Corinne Verdeil, Maria Seletskaja, Gaela Pujol und Iana Salenko
3 Mit Javier Peña Vazquez (links) und Arshak Ghalumyan

Training for the fairy Violante – Corinne Verdeil

1 Right from the coiffeur
2 Corinne Verdeil, Maria Seletskaja, Gaela Pujol and Iana Salenko
3 With Javier Peña Vazquez (left) and Arshak Ghalumyan

Zwischen Tanz und Musik –
Maria Seletskaja

1/2 Der Beginn einer Doppel-
karriere? Maria Seletskaja
auf dem Weg zur Pianistin
und Ballettdirigentin

Große Sprünge

3 Nadja Saidakova
4 Rainer Krenstetter

Between dance and music –
Maria Seletskaja

1/2 The beginning of a dual career?
Maria Seletskaja on her way
of becoming a pianist and ballet
conductor

Great leaps

3 Nadja Saidakova
4 Rainer Krenstetter

Akt 1 37

Martin Buczkó

1 Mit Wieslaw Dudek und Polina Semionova
2 Martin Buczkó

Die neue Tänzergeneration

3 Oliver Wulff (vorne), Sergej Upkin, Dmitri Boulgakov, Elena Pris, Mario Hernandez, Vladislav Marinov, David Simic, Elodie Estève, Maria Giambona und Iana Balova
4 Mario Hernandez mit Michael Banzhaf
5 Arshak Ghalumyan, Leonard Jakovina
6 Xenia Wiest, Javier Peña Vazquez

Martin Buczkó

1 With Wieslaw Dudek and Polina Semionova
2 Martin Buczkó

The new generation of dancers

3 Oliver Wulff (in front), Sergej Upkin, Dmitri Boulgakov, Elena Pris, Mario Hernandez, Vladislav Marinov, David Simic, Elodie Estève, Maria Giambona and Iana Balova
4 Mario Hernandez with Michael Banzhaf
5 Arshak Ghalumyan, Leonard Jakovina
6 Xenia Wiest, Javier Peña Vazquez

Ibrahim Önal und Sebnem Gülseker

1 Ibrahim Önal
2 Mit Arshak Ghalumyan und Leonard Jakovina
3 Mit Elana Pris und Andrej Klemm
4 Zwiesprache vor der Humboldt-universität
5 Sebnem Gülseker

Ibrahim Önal und Sebnem Gülseker

1 Ibrahim Önal
2 With Arshak Ghalumyan and Leonard Jakovina
3 With Elana Pris and Andrej Klemm
4 Dialogue in front of the Humboldt University
5 Sebnem Gülseker

Augenblicke der Enstpannung,
Augenblicke der Konzentration

Nadia Yanowsky und Wieslaw Dudek

1. Nadia Yanowsky
2. Mit Zitra
3. Wieslaw Dudek
4. Wieslaw Dudek mit Martin Buczkó und Polina Semionova
5. Wieslav Dudek, Nadja Saidakova, Arshak Ghalumyan und Leonard Jakovina
6. Nadia Yanowsky, Rainer Krenstetter

Moments of relaxation,
moments of concentration

Nadia Yanowsky and Wieslaw Dudek

1. Nadia Yanowsky
2. With Zitra
3. Wieslaw Dudek
4. Wieslaw Dudek with Martin Buczkó and Polina Semionova
5. Wieslav Dudek, Nadja Saidakova, Arshak Ghalumyan and Leonard Jakovina
6. Nadia Yanowsky, Rainer Krenstetter

Rainer Krenstetter: der Blaue Vogel privat – und in der Probe zum Pas de deux mit Prinzessin Florine

1 Mit Alessandra Pasquali
2 … und Nadia Yanowsky
3/4 Rainer Krenstetter
5 Rainer Krenstetter, Dinu Tamazlacaru und Ronald Savkovic (von vorne nach hinten)

Rainer Krenstetter: bluebird in private – and during the rehearsals for the Pas de deux with Princess Florine

1 With Alessandra Pasquali
2 … and Nadia Yanowsky
3/4 Rainer Krenstetter
5 Rainer Krenstetter, Dinu Tamazlacaru and Ronald Savkovic (from front to back)

Freundinnen – Elodie Puna und Gaela Pujol

1 Elodie Puna und Gaela Pujol
2 Elodie Puna
3 Gaela Pujol
4 Trost und vergnügte Momente beim Shopping nach Elodie Punas Arbeitsunfall
5 Elodie Puna

Friends – Elodie Puna and Gaela Pujol

1 Elodie Puna and Gaela Pujol
2 Elodie Puna
3 Gaela Pujol
4 Consolation and happy moments – comfort shopping after Elodie Puna's occupational accident
5 Elodie Puna

Ein Paar im Leben, ein Paar auf der Bühne: Marian Walter und Iana Salenko

A couple in life, a couple on stage: Marian Walter und Iana Salenko

1–3 Marian Walter und Iana Salenko
4 Iana Salenko (vorne) und Gaela Pujol
5 Iana Salenko mit Vladimir Malakhov

1–3 Marian Walter and Iana Salenko
4 Iana Salenko (in front) and Gaela Pujol
5 Iana Salenko with Vladimir Malakhov

3

Kater und Kätzchen

1 Javier Peña Vazquez
2 Artur Lill und Johanna Hwang
3 Johanna Hwang
4 Johanna Hwang (vorne), Natalia Munoz

Puss in Boots

1 Javier Peña Vazquez
2 Artur Lill and Johanna Hwang
3 Johanna Hwang
4 Johanna Hwang (in front), Natalia Munoz

4

Pas de deux in der Kunst und im Leben – Elena Pris

1 Mit Artem Shpilevsky
2 Elena Pris
3 Mit Yann Vandenhaute
4 An der Spree mit Marcin Krajewski

Pas de deux in art and in life – Elena Pris

1 With Artem Shpilevsky
2 Elena Pris
3 With Yann Vandenhaute
4 At the Spree witz Marcin Krajewski

Solistin und Ballettmeister: eine Verbindung über den Ballettsaal hinaus: Maria-Helena Buckley und Andrej Klemm

1 Andrej Klemm und Maria-Helena Buckley
2 Maria-Helena Buckley
3 Andrej Klemm mit Elena Pris und Ibrahim Önal
4/5 Maria-Helena Buckley

Soloist and Ballet master: a connection beyond the ballet studio: Maria-Helena Buckley and Andrej Klemm

1 Andrej Klemm and Maria-Helena Buckley
2 Maria-Helena Buckley
3 Andrej Klemm with Elena Pris and Ibrahim Önal
4/5 Maria-Helena Buckley

Michael Banzhaf erarbeitet sich die böse Fee Carabosse

1/6 Michael Banzhaf
2 Mit Beatrice Knop
3 Mit Ulian Topor, Yann Vandenhaute, Marcin Dempc und Dimitri Boulgakov
4 Vladimir Malakhov, Michael Banzhaf und Ronald Savkovic
5 … und abends in die Philharmonie

Michael Banzhaf is working on the evil fairy Carabosse

1/6 Michael Banzhaf
2 With Beatrice Knop
3 With Ulian Topor, Yann Vandenhaute, Marcin Dempc and Dimitri Boulgakov
4 Vladimir Malakhov, Michael Banzhaf and Ronald Savkovic
5 Let's go to the Philharmonic in the evening!

Die gute Fliederfee – Beatrice Knop

1/3 Beatrice Knop
2 Mit Vladimir Malakhov

The good Lilac Fairy – Beatrice Knop

1/3 Beatrice Knop
2 With Vladimir Malakhov

Prinz und Prinzessinnen – Artem Shpilevsky

1 Mit Polina Seminova
2 Artem Shpilevsky
3/4 Mit Elena Pris

Prince and Princesses – Artem Shpilevsky

1 With Polina Seminova
2 Artem Shpilevsky
3/4 With Elena Pris

Proben zum Grand Pas de deux
Prinzessin Aurora – Prinz Desiré

Rehearsals for the Grand Pas de
deux Princess Aurora – Prince Désiré

1/2 Polina Semionova und
Artem Shpilevsky

1/2 Polina Semionova and
Artem Shpilevsky

Akt 1 **63**

**Ein Engel in Berlin –
Polina Semionova**

1/2 Polina Semionova
3/4 Mit Ronald Savkovic

**An angel in Berlin –
Polina Semionova**

1/2 Polina Semionova
3/4 With Ronald Savkovic

Akt 1 **65**

Präzision und Hingabe:
Übungen in parallelen Rollen
als Odile und Manon

Precision and devotion:
Exercises for the parallel roles
Odile and Manon

1/2 Polina Semionova
  3 Polina Semionova und
    Ronald Savkovic

1/2 Polina Semionova
  3 Polina Semionova and
    Ronald Savkovic

Akt 1 **67**

Ronald Savkovic

1 Mit Nadja Saidakova
2 Ronald Savkovic (vorne), Mariane Joly, Michael Banzhaf, Mario Hernandez
3 Zu Besuch im jüdischen Museum Berlin

Ronald Savkovic

1 With Nadja Saidakova
2 Ronald Savkovic (in front), Mariane Joly, Michael Banzhaf, Mario Hernandez
3 A visit to the Jewish Museum in Berlin

Nadja Saidakova – eine Prinzessin
auf der Bühne … und privat mit
Familie und ihrem kleinen Prinzen

1 Mit Andrej Klemm, Birgit Brux
und Arshak Ghalumyan
2 Iana Salenko, Nadja Saidakova
und Gaela Pujol
3 Mit Ronald Savkovic
4–8 Mit Sohn Bogdan und Andrej

Nadja Saidakova – a princess
on the stage … and in private with
her family and her little prince

1 With Andrej Klemm, Birgit
Brux and Arshak Ghalumyan
2 Iana Salenko, Nadja Saidakova
and Gaela Pujol
3 With Ronald Savkovic
4–8 With son Bogdan and Andrej

Valentina Savina, die Erste Ballettmeisterin, teilt ihren großen Erfahrungsschatz mit den Solisten

1/2 Mit Ronald Savkovic
3 Mit Vladimir Malakhov und Michael Banzhaf
4 Valentina Savina

Valentina Savina, the principal ballet mistress, shares the wealth of her experiences with the soloists

1/2 With Ronald Savkovic
3 With Vladimir Malakhov and Michael Banzhaf
4 Valentina Savina

3

4

Akt 1 **73**

Momentaufnahmen	Snap-shots
1 Vladislav Marinov beim Studium der Probendisposition	1 Vladislav Marinov, studying the rehearsal schedule
2 Birgit Brux und Nadja Saidakova	2 Birgit Brux and Nadja Saidakova
3 Nanami Terai und Maria Giambona	3 Nanami Terai and Maria Giambona
4 Vladislav Marinov	4 Vladislav Marinov
5 Dirigent Alexander Sotnikov	5 Conductor Alexander Sotnikov
6 Aoi Suyama	6 Aoi Suyama

Akt 1 **75**

Vladimir Malakhov …

1 … der Intendant …
2 … der Choreograph, hier mit
  der Ballettmeisterin Christine
  Camillo, …
3–5 … und der Tänzer, rechts unten
  mit Michael Banzhaf

Vladimir Malakhov …

1 … the Artistic Director …
2 … the choreographer, here
  with the ballet mistress
  Christine Camillo, …
3–5 … and the dancer, below right
  with Michael Banzhaf

Akt 1 **77**

Akt 2

**Umzug in das Haus
in der Bismarckstraße**

1/2 Erste Proben auf der Bühne
der Deutschen Oper Berlin
3 Leonard Jakovina
4 Elodie Estève, Verena Thurm,
Emi Hariyama, Iana Balova

**Moving into the opera
at Bismarckstrasse**

1/2 First rehearsals on the stage
of the Berlin Deutsche Oper
3 Leonard Jakovina
4 Elodie Estève, Verena Thurm,
Emi Hariyama, Iana Balova

Die ›Dornenhecke‹ – noch ohne Dornen

1 Polina Semionova
2 Vladimir Malakhov
3 Diana Vishneva und Michael Banzhaf
4 Diana Vishneva
5 Michael Banzhaf

The "thorn hedge" – still without thorns

1 Polina Semionova
2 Vladimir Malakhov
3 Diana Vishneva and Michael Banzhaf
4 Diana Vishneva
5 Michael Banzhaf

Akt 2 **83**

Eindrücke von der Probenarbeit

1 Nanami Terai
2 Iana Salenko
3 Vladmir Malakhov
4 Valentina Savina

Impressions of the rehearsals

1 Nanami Terai
2 Iana Salenko
3 Vladmir Malakhov
4 Valentina Savina

Für Langeweile keine Zeit: Spitzen-schuhe müssen vorbereitet werden

1 Nadja Saidakova und ihr Sohn
  Bogdan
2 Nadia Yanowsky
3 Diana Vishneva, Sebnem Gülseker
4 Gaela Pujol und Iana Salenko

No time for boredom: pointe shoes have to be prepared

1 Nadja Saidakova and her son
  Bogdan
2 Nadia Yanowsky
3 Diana Vishneva, Sebnem Gülseker
4 Gaela Pujol and Iana Salenko

Pause: Momente der Ruhe, Ablenkung und Entspannung

1 Elodie Puna hat sich verletzt und wird zur Premiere nicht tanzen
2 Christian Krehl und Sven Seidelmann
3 Tänzers liebstes Schuhwerk
4 Physiotherapeutin Sabine Müller mit Artem Shpilevsky
5 Marianne Klig
6 Nadia Yanowsky, Dariusz Prill und Marcin Dempc

Break: moments of rest, distraction and relaxation

1 Elodie Puna will not dance the premiere due to a stage accident
2 Christian Krehl and Sven Seidelmann
3 A dancer's favourite footwear
4 Physiotherapist Sabine Müller with Artem Shpilevsky
5 Marianne Klig
6 Nadia Yanowsky, Dariusz Prill and Marcin Dempc

1

2

Starke Frauen

1 Elena Pris
2 Beatrice Knop
3 Ronald Savkovic und
  Nadja Saidakova
4 Maria Seletskaja

Notable women

1 Elena Pris
2 Beatrice Knop
3 Ronald Savkovic and
  Nadja Saidakova
4 Maria Seletskaja

Akt 2 **91**

Kostümprobe – Valery Kungurov ist verantwortlich für Rosen, Dornen und all die bunte Farbenpracht

1 Iana Salenko
2 Valery Kungurov
3 Vladimir Malakhov
4 Die Kostümdirektion der Deutschen Oper Berlin im Einsatz: Dorothea Katzer, Anke Riedel, Kerstin Berner, Polina Semionova und Valery Kungurov
5 Polina Semionova

Costume fitting – Valery Kungurov is responsible for roses, thorns and the entire colourful splendour

1 Iana Salenko
2 Valery Kungurov
3 Vladimir Malakhov
4 The costume directors of the Berlin Deutsche Oper in action: Dorothea Katzer, Anke Riedel, Kerstin Berner, Polina Semionova and Valery Kungurov
5 Polina Semionova

Akt 2 **93**

Ein häuserübergreifendes Projekt: Lagebesprechung in den Kostüm-werkstätten der Staatsoper Berlin

1 Polina Semionova
2 Die Kostümdirektorin der Staatsoper Berlin, Hannelore Wedermeÿer, Karin Merten und Vladimir Malakhov
3 Vladimir Malakhov
4 Polina Semionova

A project spanning several opera houses: briefing in the wardrobes of the Berlin State Opera

1 Polina Semionova
2 The costume director of the Berlin State Opera, Hannelore Wedermeÿer, Karin Merten and Vladimir Malakhov
3 Vladimir Malakhov
4 Polina Semionova

Akt 2 **95**

Feenzauber

1 Elena Pris
2 Gaela Pujol und Elodie Puna
3 Iana Salenko

Magic of the fairies

1 Elena Pris
2 Gaela Pujol and Elodie Puna
3 Iana Salenko

Akt 2 **97**

Metamorphosen

1 Ronald Savkovic verwandelt sich in die böse Fee Carabosse
2 Ohne Schminkspiegel und Pinsel geht gar nichts: Iana Salenko
3 Beatrice Knop
4 Nadja Saidakova

Metamorphoses

1 Ronald Savkovic turns into the evil fairy Carabosse
2 Nothing comes without make-up mirror and brush: Iana Salenko
3 Beatrice Knop
4 Nadja Saidakova

Akt 2 **99**

Monster, die Begleiter der Carabosse

1 Ulian Topor
2/5 Dmitri Boulgakov
3 Marian Lazar
4 Mario Hernandez
6 Ulian Topor und Maskenbildner Udo Konrad

Monsters, the companions of Carabosse

1 Ulian Topor
2/5 Dmitri Boulgakov
3 Marian Lazar
4 Mario Hernandez
6 Ulian Topor and make-up man Udo Konrad

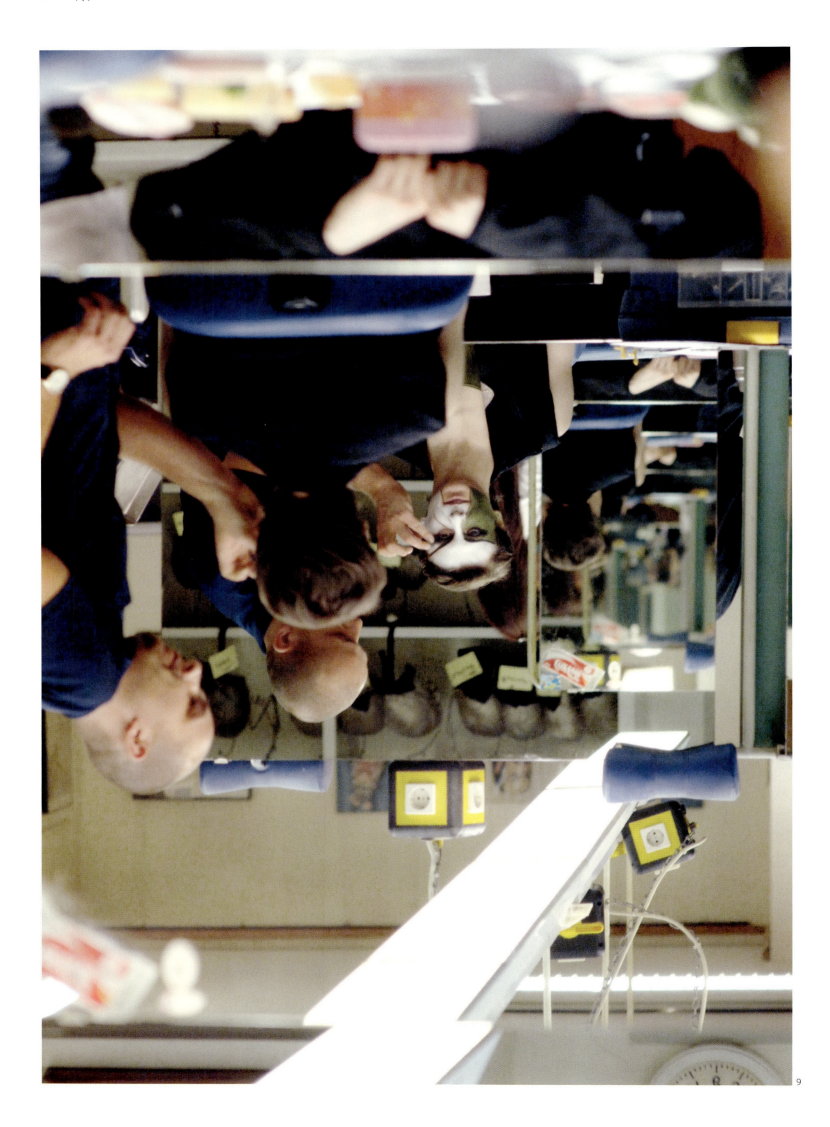

Augenblicke

1 Oliver Wulff
2 Michael Banzhaf
3 Oliver Wulff und Emily Archer
4 Barbara Schroeder
5 Beatrice Knop

Moments

1 Oliver Wulff
2 Michael Banzhaf
3 Oliver Wulff and Emily Archer
4 Barbara Schroeder
5 Beatrice Knop

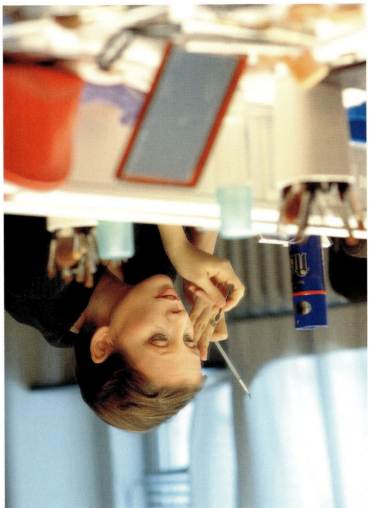

Die letzten Handgriffe in der Garderobe

1 Elena Pris
2 Ibrahim Önal
3 Birgit Brux
4 Gaela Pujol

The last moves in the dressing room

1 Elena Pris
2 Ibrahim Önal
3 Birgit Brux
4 Gaela Pujol

Gespannte Aufmerksamkeit vor der ersten Hauptprobe

1 Sven Seidelmann
2 Sebnem Gülseker
3 Robert Wohlert
4 Artur Lill
5 Yann Vandenhaute

Rapt attention before the first dress rehearsal

1 Sven Seidelmann
2 Sebnem Gülseker
3 Robert Wohlert
4 Artur Lill
5 Yann Vandenhaute

Beim Eintanzen, wenige Minuten vor der Vorstellung

1/4 Polina Semionova
2 Nadia Yanowsky
3 Brenda Saleh

Warm-up routine a few minutes before the performance

1/4 Polina Semionova
2 Nadia Yanowsky
3 Brenda Saleh

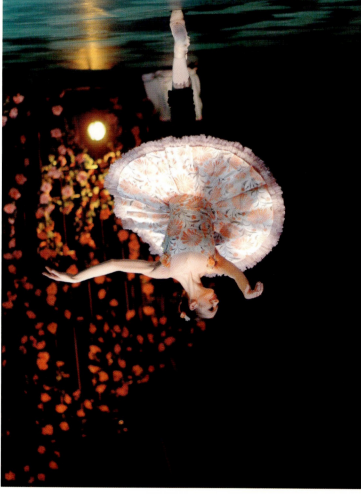

Die Nervosität steigt

1 Maria-Helena Buckley
2 Diana Vishneva
3 Artur Lill

The nervousness is increasing

1 Maria-Helena Buckley
2 Diana Vishneva
3 Artur Lill

Akt 3

König und Königin

1/2 Birgit Brux
3 Alexander Chmelnitzky
4 Birgit Brux

King and Queen

1/2 Birgit Brux
3 Alexander Chmelnitzky
4 Birgit Brux

Die guten Feen

1. Elena Pris (Fée Candide),
   Beatrice Knop (Fée des Lilas),
   Corinne Verdeil (Fée Violante)
2. Iana Salenko (Fée Canari qui chante)
3. Beatrice Knop (Fée des Lilas)
4. Sebnem Güseker (Fée Miettes qui tombent)

The good fairies

1. Elena Pris (Fée Candide),
   Beatrice Knop (Fée des Lilas),
   Corinne Verdeil (Fée Violante)
2. Iana Salenko (Fée Canari qui chante)
3. Beatrice Knop (Fée des Lilas)
4. Sebnem Güseker (Fée Miettes qui tombent)

Die Feen tanzen für Prinzessin Aurora

1 Beatrice Knop
2 Sebnem Gülseker, Elena Pris, Iana Salenko, Beatrice Knop, Corinne Verdeil, Gaela Pujol
3 Iana Salenko

The fairies dance for Princess Aurora

1 Beatrice Knop
2 Sebnem Gülseker, Elena Pris, Iana Salenko, Beatrice Knop, Corinne Verdeil, Gaela Pujol
3 Iana Salenko

Der Einbruch der dunklen Mächte in die Idylle

1–5 Carabosse (Michael Banzhaf) inmitten ihrer Monster und als Gegenspieler der Fliederfee

Evil is invading the idyll

1–5 Carabosse (Michael Banzhaf) in the midst of her monsters and as antagonist of the Lilac Fairy

Eine Demütigung mit Folgen

1–4 Hofzeremonienmeister Catalabutte (Oliver Wulff) kann die rasende Carabosse (Michael Banzhaf) nicht beruhigen

Humiliation with consequences

1–4 The Master of Ceremonies Catalabutte (Oliver Wulff) cannot calm down the raging Carabosse (Michael Banzhaf)

Charakterstudien der bösen Feen

1–5 Michael Banzhaf
     als Carabosse

Character studies of the evil fairy

1–5 Michael Banzhaf
     as Carabosse

Fest-Szenen

1 Katharina Mende und David Simic
2 Auroras Freundinnen und Prinzen
3 Emi Hariyama
4 Alessandra Pasquali
5 Schlusspose des Walzers

Scenes of festivity

1 Katharina Mende and David Simic
2 Aurora's friends and princes
3 Emi Hariyama
4 Alessandra Pasquali
5 Final pose of the waltz

Die kleine Aurora mit einem Fabergé-Ei ahnt nichts von dem Ringen zwischen Fliederfee und Carabosse um ihr Leben

1 Juliette Johnson
2 Beatrice Knop
3 Michal Banzhaf

Little Aurora with a Fabergé egg has no premonition of the fight between the Lilac Fairy and Carabosse for her life

1 Juliette Johnson
2 Beatrice Knop
3 Michal Banzhaf

1 Juliette Johnson

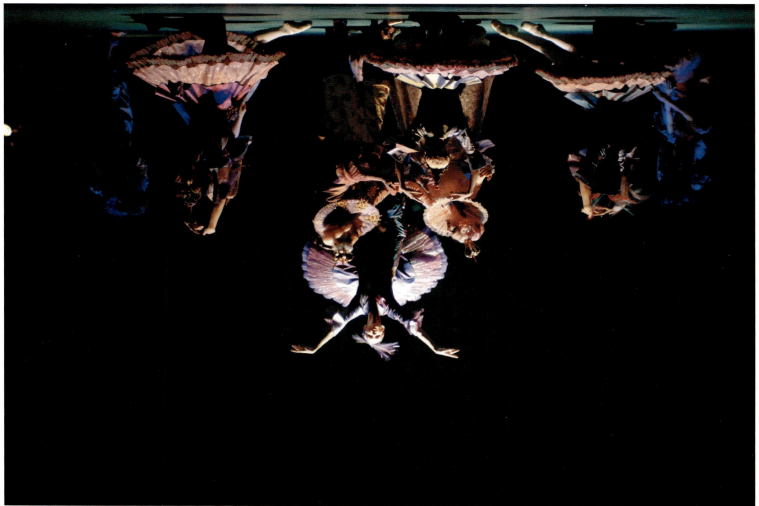

Geburtstag der herangewachsenen
Prinzessin Aurora: Szenen aus dem
Rosenadagio |

1 Diana Vishneva
2 Alexander Chmelnitzky
 und Diana Vishneva
3 Diana Vishneva
4 Oliver Wulff

Birthday of the grown-up
Princess Aurora: Scenes from
the Rose Adagio |

1 Diana Vishneva
2 Alexander Chmelnitzky
 and Diana Vishneva
3 Diana Vishneva
4 Oliver Wulff

Szenen aus dem Rosenadagio II

1. Diana Vishneva, Brenda Saleh, Ibrahim Önal und Barbara Schroeder
2. Diana Vishneva
3. Diana Vishneva und Martin Buczkó
4. Diana Vishneva

Scenes from the Rose Adagio II

1. Diana Vishneva, Brenda Saleh, Ibrahim Önal and Barbara Schroeder
2. Diana Vishneva
3. Diana Vishneva and Martin Buczkó
4. Diana Vishneva

Die Geburtstagsszene in einer alternativen Besetzung

1 Nadja Saidakova mit Sarah Mestrovic, Nanami Terai, Wieslav Dudek und Ibrahim Önal
2 Nadja Saidakova mit Ibrahim Önal
3 Nadja Saidakova
4 Die verhängnisvolle Rose: Michael Banzhaf mit Nadja Saidakova

The birthday scene with an alternative cast

1 Nadja Saidakova with Sarah Mestrovic, Nanami Terai, Wieslav Dudek and Ibrahim Önal
2 Nadja Saidakova with Ibrahim Önal
3 Nadja Saidakova
4 The fatal rose: Michael Banzhaf with Nadja Saidakova

Akt 3 139

1 Die schlafende Schöne,
behütet von den Feen
2–4 Beatrice Knop
5 Ein Traum von Rettung:
Vladimir Malakhov, Diana
Vishneva und Beatrice Knop

Die Fliederfee beschützt Aurora
und verwandelt den Tod in hundertjährigen Schlaf

1 La Belle dormant, protected
by the fairies
2–4 Beatrice Knop
5 A dream of salvation: Vladimir
Malakhov, Diana Vishneva and
Beatrice Knop

The Lilac Fairy protects Aurora
and changes the death sentence
into 100 years of sleep

Der Auftritt des Prinzen Désiré

1–3 Vladimir Malakhov
 4 Vladimir Malakhov
   mit Iana Salenko
 5 Vladimir Malakhov

Prince Désiré appears

1–3 Vladimir Malakhov
 4 Vladimir Malakho
   with Iana Salenko
 5 Vladimir Malakhov

Akt 3 143

Die Vision des Prinzen Désiré

1 Polina Semionova
2/3 Diana Vishneva
4 Polina Semionova und Artem Shpilevsky

The vision of Prince Désiré

1 Polina Semionova
2/3 Diana Vishneva
4 Polina Semionova and Artem Shpilevsky

1 Diana Vishneva und
  Vladimir Malakhov
2 Diana Vishneva
3 Beatrice Knop und
  Vladimir Malakhov

Prinz Désiré träumt von Aurora,
die Fliederfee weist ihm den Weg

1 Diana Vishneva and
  Vladimir Malakhov
2 Diana Vishneva
3 Beatrice Knop and
  Vladimir Malakhov

Prince Désiré dreams of Aurora,
the Lilac Fairy shows him the way

Divertissements: Cinderella mit Prinz Fortuné und der Auftritt der Edelsteine

1 Fliederfee (Beatrice Knop)
2/3 Aschenbrödel und Prinz Fortuné (Alessandra Pasquali, Leonard Jakovina)
4 Diamant (Viara Natcheva)

Divertissements: Cinderella with Prince Fortuné and the appearance of the Gemstones

1 The Lilac Fairy (Beatrice Knop)
2/3 Cinderella and Prince Fortuné (Alessandra Pasquali, Leonard Jakovina)
4 Diamond (Viara Natcheva)

Pas de deux: Der blaue Vogel und Prinzessin Florine

1–3 Rainer Krenstetter und Nadia Yanowsky

Fliederfee

4/5 Beatrice Knop

Pas de deux: Bluebird and Princess Florine

1–3 Rainer Krenstetter and Nadia Yanowsky

Lilac Fairy

4/5 Beatrice Knop

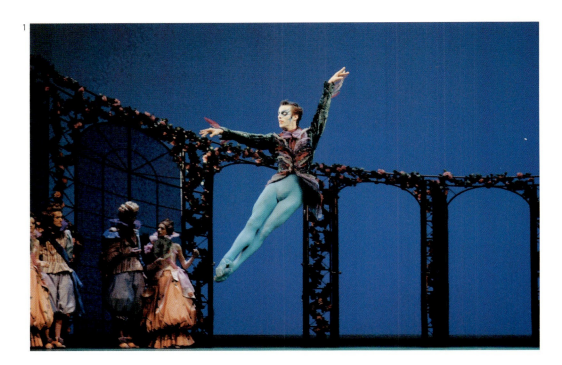

Cinderella und Prinz Fortuné
1 Leonard Jakovina und
 Alessandra Pasquali
2 Johanna Hwang
3/4 Johanna Hwang und Artur Lill

Kater und Kätzchen

Cinderella and Prince Fortuné
1 Leonard Jakovina and
 Alessandra Pasquali
2 Johanna Hwang
3/4 Johanna Hwang and Artur Lill

Puss in Boots

Grand Pas de deux:
Prinzessin Aurora und Prinz Désiré

1 Polina Semionova und Artem Shpilevsky
2/3 Diana Vishneva und Vladimir Malakhov

Grand Pas de deux:
Princess Aurora and Prince Désiré

1 Polina Semionova and Artem Shpilevsky
2/3 Diana Vishneva and Vladimir Malakhov

Vladimir Malakhov und sein Ensemble verbeugen sich vor dem Berliner Publikum

1 Die Feen: Iana Salenko, Gaela Pujol, Elena Pris, Corinne Verdeil, Sebnem Gülseker
2 Die Edelsteine: Saphir (Stephanie Greenwald), Rubin (Maria-Helena Buckley), Diamant (Viara Natcheva) und Smaragd (Nanami Terai)
3 Michael Banzhaf, Diana Vishneva, Vladimir Malakhov, Beatrice Knop, Elena Pris, Nadia Yanowsky
4 Alexander Sotnikov, Marzena Sobanska, Diana Vishneva, Christine Camillo, Vladimir Malakhov, Monika Lubitz, Beatrice Knop und Valentina Savina

Vladimir Malakhov and his ensemble bow to the Berlin audience

1 The fairies: Iana Salenko, Gaela Pujol, Elena Pris, Corinne Verdeil, Sebnem Gülseker
2 The Gem fairies: Sapphire (Stephanie Greenwald), Ruby (Maria-Helena Buckley), Diamond (Viara Natcheva) and Emerald (Nanami Terai)
3 Michael Banzhaf, Diana Vishneva, Vladimir Malakhov, Beatrice Knop, Elena Pris, Nadia Yanowsky
4 Alexander Sotnikov, Marzena Sobanska, Diana Vishneva, Christine Camillo, Vladimir Malakhov, Monika Lubitz, Beatrice Knop und Valentina Savina

Backstage nach der Vorstellung

1 Diana Vishneva und Vladimir Malakhov
2 Diana Vishneva und Alexander Sotnikov
3 Vladimir Malakhov und Valery Kungurov
4 Valentina Savina und Iana Salenko

Backstage after the performance

1 Diana Vishneva and Vladimir Malakhov
2 Diana Vishneva and Alexander Sotnikov
3 Vladimir Malakhov and Valery Kungurov
4 Valentina Savina and Iana Salenko

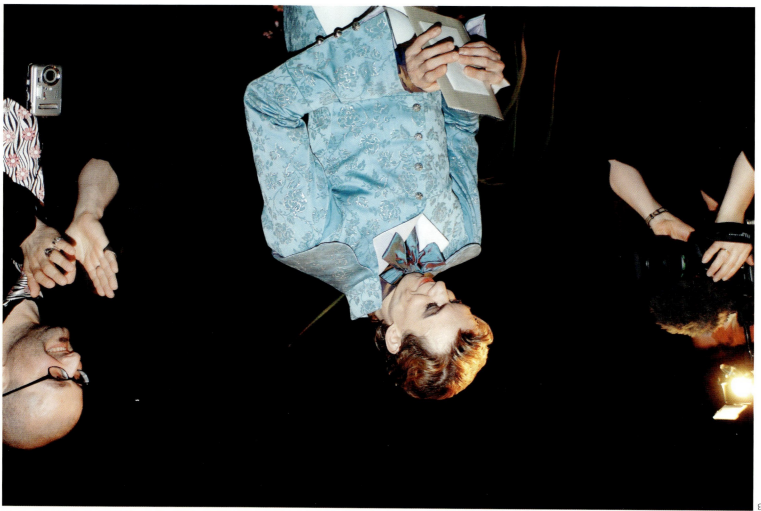

Abgeschminkt, die Maske fällt

1/2 Michael Banzhaf
3 Birgit Brux

The make-up is removed, the mask drops

1/2 Michael Banzhaf
3 Birgit Brux

4.10 Uhr: Berlin Prenzlauer Berg, bei Michael Banzhaf. Die Premierennacht weicht dem nahenden Morgen; nächstes Training 10.15 Uhr

4.10 a.m.: Berlin Prenzlauer Berg, at the home of Michael Banzhaf. The premiere night gives way to morning. Next training at 10.15 a.m.